THE HISTORICAL NOVEL

THE HISTORICAL
NOVEL ❧ AN ESSAY
BY H. BUTTERFIELD
FELLOW OF PETERHOUSE

 CAMBRIDGE: AT
THE UNIVERSITY
PRESS : MCMXXIV

CAMBRIDGE UNIVERSITY PRESS
Cambridge, New York, Melbourne, Madrid, Cape Town,
Singapore, São Paulo, Delhi, Tokyo, Mexico City

Cambridge University Press
The Edinburgh Building, Cambridge CB2 8RU, UK

Published in the United States of America by Cambridge University Press, New York

www.cambridge.org
Information on this title: www.cambridge.org/9781107650091

First published 1924
First paperback edition 2011

A catalogue record for this publication is available from the British Library

ISBN 978-1-107-65009-1 Paperback

PREFACE

THE following essay, which was awarded the Le Bas Prize for 1923, is an attempt to find some relation between historical novels on the one hand and history treated as a study on the other; and, further, to work out a method of critical approach. It does not defend historical fiction against the historian; it welcomes this form of art from his point of view, finding its justification in the character of history itself. It seeks to estimate the novel as a work of resurrection, a form of "history," a way of treating the past. In this it does not pretend to be exhaustive, but puts forward one aspect of the problem and attempts to track down the peculiar virtue of fiction as the gateway to the past.

H. B.

April 1924

I

WORDSWORTH touches the true mood of romantic regret when he writes

> "*Of old, unhappy, far-off things,*
> *And battles long ago.*"

These words call us to the window that opens out upon the past, and they set the mind thinking in pictures; for the mind of every one of us holds a jumble of pictures and stories, shot through, perhaps with sentiment, that constitute what we have built up for ourselves of the Past, and are always ready to be called into play by a glimpse of some old ruin that awakens fine associations, or by a hint of the romantic, such as Wordsworth gives in those lines. A cathedral bell, or the mention of Agincourt, or the very spelling of the word "ycleped" may be enough to send the mind wandering into its own picture-galleries of history, just as the words "Once upon a time—" waft us into the realms of fairy-story; these things are symbols, keys that unlock a world in our minds. Let a Pre-Raphaelite picture remind us of lost fashions or a schoolboy sing "John Peel" and we are bridging the centuries; and only a few key-words are needed to give the mind a clue, and we are with the Elizabethans on the Spanish Main, or with King Harold, defending the gate of England.

A hundred things have helped to build up this picture-gallery of history—not merely history-books, but Bible-stories, and local traditions and stories from opera; not merely biographies but the border-ballads that the old gipsies would sing amid grim surroundings, and the rant of politicians who talk of Magna Carta or Nelson, and the picturesque advertisements of magazines and street-posters; out of all these there has grown up a world in our minds and that world is what we make for ourselves of the past. We may try to modify and correct it by our conscious studies, but we cannot escape it. And not the least of the sources of it is the Historical Novel.

Sir Walter Scott did not write historical novels because he wished to teach history in an easy way or to get at a moral indirectly, but because his mind was full of the past, just as the mind of a musician is full of tunes; he made for himself a world out of the past, and lived in it much; and he painted that world for his readers, and turned it into a tale. Whatever connection the historical novel may have with the history that men write and build up out of their conscious studies, or with History, the past as it really happened, the thing that is the object of study and research, it certainly has something to do with that world, that mental picture which each of us makes of the past; it helps our imagination to build up its idea of the past. After all the history we have ever learned our first thought of Mediaeval England is quite likely to be a picture of England as the setting for Ivanhoe and Robin Hood, even if our second thought is that this is all wrong; and though we may not seek to gather our historical facts from the novel, there are more subtle things, unconscious prejudices and unformulated sentiments that we take in unawares, there are pictures that haunt us, there is an atmosphere that compels us, and if we find nothing else we find the sentiment of history, the feeling for the past, in the historical novel. On one side, therefore, the historical novel is a "form" of history. It is a way of treating the past.

In this it is linked up with legend, and the traditions of localities, and popular ballads; like these it goes beyond the authenticated data of history-books, the definitely recoverable things of the past, in order to paint its picture and tell its story; and like these it often subordinates fidelity to the recovered facts of history, and strict accuracy of detail, to some other kind of effectiveness. And these legends and popular stories are related to the historical novel in a way similar to that in which a snatch of folk-song is related to the music of a cultured genius, or an anecdote or a piece of gossip is related to some work of structure as well as of fiction, like the novel. The one is a work of apparently popular, or at least anonymous origin, the other is a deliberately artistic and organised production. When we hear those legends we feel that it is Earth itself that throws them out; it is this old World of ours telling a tale that she seems to remember. These things ask to be believed; a local tradition claims to be true, or it has no currency; but the historical novel is conscious in its purpose and in its inventions. We do not say that we enjoy it "although" it is not quite true to facts; the element of fiction in it is avowed, and is part of the intention of the work; for the historical novel is a "form" of fiction as well as of history. It is a tale, a piece of invention; only, it claims to be true to the life of the past.

And so there is a double set of relations to be considered in any study of the subject, arising out of the double character of the subject. On one side the historical novel may be regarded simply as a novel with a particular kind of background; a story set, say, in the Middle Ages, just as a novel of modern times might find its setting in some far country. But if this were the whole truth of the matter there would be no point in giving it a special study. A fairy-tale is not merely an ordinary kind of story set in fairy-land, but becomes a different kind of story by being placed there; in the same way, although in a sense every novel tends to become in time a historical novel, and there will come a day when "Sonia" will be useful to the historian for a certain kind of information, yet a true "historical novel" is one that is historical in its intention and not simply by accident, one that comes from a mind steeped in the past. Such a novel will have a special kind of appeal.

When a composer picks up a piece of poetry and puts it to music he weaves a web of invention around the words and amplifies them with something that belongs to an art different from their own; in doing so he will probably alter the swing of the poem and create rhythms of his own, and in the music that he makes the original music of the words themselves will almost certainly be destroyed; even when he is trying to interpret the poem he may be changing its very character, making a breezy thing desolate, or converting a majestic hymn into a joyful anthem, and, unawares, he may be doing everything that would send the poet crazy, and make men of letters indignant. The final result may not be good as poetry, may indeed be a good piece of poetry spoilt in the very things that make it good, the character of the original words having been altered in a hundred subtle ways. Standing alone it may not even be a good piece of music exactly. But it may be what it sets out to be—a good piece of work in a form neither poetry nor music, but a combination of the two, a new creation, something with an appeal of its own. That is to say, it may be a good piece of song, that justifies itself when it comes from the voice of the singer.

Like an opera, in which music and poetry and drama melt into one another to produce what amounts to a new kind of art, with a purpose and an idiom of its own; like a song, in which music and poetry are interlocked, and become one harmony, the historical novel is a fusion. It is one of the arts that are born of the marriage of different arts. A historical event is "put to fiction" as a poem is put to music; it is turned into story as words are turned into song; it is put into a context of narrative which is like the result that is obtained when words are printed between the staves of a vocal score. And just as a composer in choosing a poem to set to music, accepts certain limitations, volunteers a certain allegiance, and must in some way be loyal to the poetry he has selected, so the historical novelist owes a certain loyalty to the history of which he treats. But because this is a marriage of the arts it is not a complete loyalty, and just as poets complain because musicians modify the original rhythms of their poems and the lilt of the words, so historians cry out because a Scott tampers with history. For all arts that combine different forms of art are beset with divided loyalties like these, and with causes of disagreement and annoyance. The very appeal that they should make is a thing to be discovered, a matter of controversy. And in the study of them, every issue is a complicated one.

And, lastly, it may be said that a given song

may be good poetry if read in an armchair; the
music of a song may be good in itself if played
over on some instrument; and yet the song may
be a poor thing when sung by anybody, if the
two do not hang together, if the marriage is not
a harmony. In the same way, a historical novel
may be a good book but not a good historical
novel. It may be a just piece of history; or it
may be a good story; but it may not be good with
the special goodness of a historical novel, it
may not combine its two elements in just the
way that is needed. It is not exactly that history
and fiction should dovetail into one another to
produce a coherent whole; it is not simply that
the story of the Popish Plot can be rounded off
by a piece of invention, or the tragedy of Mary
Queen of Scots depicted more fully and with
more connectedness by the interspersion of
imaginary episodes; but it is rather that in the
historical novel history and fiction can enrich
and amplify one another, and interpenetrate.
They can grow into one another, each making
the other more powerful. And they can make
a special kind of appeal to the reader.

    *   *   *   *

The facts of the past, the stuff out of which
men write their Histories, are used for many
things besides the manufacture of history. The
economist, the politician, the musician, the
ecclesiastic—in fact, specialists of all sorts, have
their own use for the facts that make up history;

they make themselves more expert in their special departments by studying the historical side of those departments, but they are not historians any more than is the architect who tries to make himself a better architect by finding out how houses used to be ventilated. The theorist makes his generalisations out of the facts of the past, and talks about the laws that govern the movements of history and the things that determine progress and the goal to which human development is moving—but he is not a historian any more than the priest talking about Providence is a historian, although both these deal with interpretations of history. They are simply philosophers trying to interpret man's experience of life to man. The Historian's interest in the past is not the economist's or the philosopher's interest in it, he loves the past for its own sake and tries to live in it, tries to live over again the lost life of yesterday, turning it back as one would turn back the pages of a book to re-read what has gone before; and he seeks to see the past as a far-country and to think himself into a different world. And so the use that he makes of the accumulated facts that tell about the past, is to recapture a bygone age and turn it into something that is at once a picture and a story.

History, then, means the world looking back upon itself, and storing up memories that are pictures. History is any tale that the old world

can tell when it starts remembering. It is just
the world's Memory.

The love of the past for its own sake, and the
fondness for lingering over those things that
endure as relics or as symbols of the past, and the
regret for the things that are lost for ever are
what one might call romanticism. Gibbon and
Gregorovius had this feeling when the sight of
the splendid ruins and remains of Rome drove
them, each in turn, to look into the story that
lay behind monument and masonry, and to
be writers of history. All of us have this feeling
when the glimpse of some historic town, or the
impressive sternness of an old castle, or the
sight of a Roman wall, awakens a world in our
minds, and sets us thinking on all the tales that
stone could tell if only it could speak the history
that it stores. These buildings and remains are
the maimed survivals, the broken emblems, of
a vivid thrilling life that has been lived, and
that we love to look back upon. Distance lends
enchantment, and the things of long-ago draw
us with their strangeness, and with a far-away,
picturesque glamour that surrounds them; and
there is just the escape that we seek from modern
life, in the possibility that we have of thinking
ourselves into a different world, which we can
suffuse with a romantic glow and which we can
think of as having more colour and adventure
than our own world. But, most of all, the reason
why we love the ruins of an abbey, and preserve

the flags that are riddled with the bullets of Waterloo—the reason why we prize the book in the margins of which Coleridge himself scribbled pencil-notes of literary criticism, and keep a lock of Keats's hair, is that these things are like the stray flowers that cheat the scythe or like the last stars that outdare the morning sun; they are the few things that are saved from a ship-wreck. The work of a historian is to reconstruct the past out of the debris that is cast up by the sea from the wrecks of countless ages.

Romanticism is at bottom a sigh for the things that perish, and the things that can never happen again. It is like the soldier going over the hill to fight, but always looking back and lingering. The things that Time destroys we love with a love fed by romantic regret—the sunset that will never just happen again, the snows of yester-year, the beliefs that are being sapped, the days of our own childhood. In *The Cloister and the Hearth*, Gerard at the beginning of his wanderings is kindly treated by a woman and her husband; as he leaves them they wish him "God speed," and, says the author, "with that they parted, and never met again in this world"; and nobody can read that sentence without loving these people more. If some novelists had described this incident, if, say Dickens had been writing this, it would have been part of his way of working, it would have been in keeping with his avowed theories of life, to renew the connection between Gerard and his kind acquaintances later in life, and by some coincidence to make the good woman and her husband turn up when we had forgotten their existence. But Reade not only declines to do this, he goes out of his way, beforehand, to tell us that he is not going to do this; he makes these people pass out into the darkness and so he leaves us with a feeling of affectionate regret for them. When we know a thing must die, something comes to reinforce our love for it, and if we were all told to take our last look upon this earth to-morrow, what worst of world-haters would not ask again and again for "just one peep more"? Universal literature is full of regrets for all the lovely things that die. All history is full of movements that are born of romantic reactions—of prophets stoned on one day and mourned the next, of rejected leaders idolised when they have passed off the stage and soon carried to power again by a mad romantic impulse that moves the people, of kings beheaded and then loved when they have become a memory, of Restorations, of returns from Elba, and of Jacobite risings. Every generation cries that the world is going to the dogs and that things are not as they have been, and two years before the Spanish Armada was routed an Englishman could complain that English courage was on the wane. All this is romanticism; and it is romanticism that makes old men gather round a chimney-corner to tell a tale of old times, and makes hardened heroes love to fight their battles over again. It is this feeling that sends us treading again the haunts of childhood and recapturing childhood scenes; that makes our imagination play around historic sites and ancient buildings, peopling them with a life that we have invented, and awaking them to their former activeness; and that so thrills the heart with a sense of the great bygone things, that some men cannot see the sun go down red without dreaming of battles long ago, till the moors become alive with excited horsemen and with noises that the hills turn into echoes, and the past seems to unearth itself.

It is possible to imagine a political theorist visiting Brazil to make a study of political conditions there; or to think of a student of public health going to Edinburgh to gain a knowledge of its drainage system; but apart from these specialists there is the traveller who will describe Brazil to men as a strange country, and there is the Stevenson who will give a sketch of Edinburgh for the general reader; and the historian is like these. He travels the past in a caravan; he dips into it as one would dip into Edinburgh, peeping into the shadowy slums and crooked streets, and hunting the eternal human things. He describes the past not because it has connections with the present that can be worked out, not because it holds a moral for to-day, but precisely because it is a strange land, precisely because it is past, and can never happen again; and he seeks to paint life as a whole—not man on his economic side, or man as a political animal, but man in all his adventures in living. Specialists and theorists may tread at his heels to draw a moral or to make generalisations, but as for the romantic historian, his is the mad human longing to see and to know people, to feel with them, and to peep at the world they lived in, and to understand their ways, their humours, their loves and fears. As he looks to the deserted ruins of a hillside farm he wonders what sentiments filled the hearts of men and women there when Jacobite rebels rode past on their dismal return Northwards; when he sees the old mill, where the tossing hill-streams meet and the twisted roads come to a ford, he wonders what difference it made to the children playing at the water's edge, when Cromwell and his troopers passed that way; and when he stands in the shadow of what was once a frowning wall, he asks himself all the things that the wall must have overheard and over-looked, and all the tales of joy and adventure, of trouble and of treachery, that it might tell if it were not doomed to keep them to itself. And once the romanticist has stared at this pro-gramme of his, and has confessed his faith and has faced himself with this thing that he is really seeking—once he has understood his heart's longing, then there must flash upon him the tremendous truth—the impossibility of history.

To the politician, the important movements and striking decisions and big crises that for him are "history," are things within reach; the military man has not much difficulty in recovering the noisy things that for him are "history"; the diplomatist knows where to look for the story of international tangles, and the mysteries of pacts and treaties and the hidden sources of power in a state; court and camp and parliament house are rich with documents and records; the things that are played out in the limelight, the stately public events are, in a way, simple to the historian, and the men who talk of democracies and regiments and alliances, and who think of people in the mass and can find food in statistics and budgets—these can discuss the condition of England and the welfare of the people. But they are far from life. Now the "huts where poor men lie" elude the world's Memory. The ploughman whom Gray saw, plodding his weary way, the rank and file of Monmouth's rebel crowd—every man of them a world in himself, a mystery of personality, more wonderful than a star—the tavern-keepers whom Puritan England strove to root out—these have left no memorial and all that we know about them is just enough to set us guessing and wondering. The things by which we re-

member an old friend—his peculiar laugh, his
way of drawing his hand through his hair, his
whistle in the street, his humour, and the sound
of his footstep on the stair—these things, at any
rate, we cannot hope to recapture in history,
any more than we can recapture last night's
sunset, or hear again a song sung by Jenny Lind.
The most homely and intimate and personal
things slip through the hands of the historian.
The history that the romanticist in us longs for,
the desire to touch the pulsing heart of men who
toyed with the world as we do, and left it long
ago, is the quest for the most elusive thing in
the world. We who cannot know our own
friends, save in a fragmentary way and at
occasional moments of self-revelation, cannot
hope to read the hearts of half-forgotten kings.
We cannot hope to get close to the lives of
humble men who trod silently through the
world. These we cannot fasten upon at all;
history is thwarted; Earth cannot remember.

History can only make her pictures and
rebuild the past out of the things she can save
from a shipwreck; she will piece together just
so much of the battle of Agincourt as the sea
washes up to the shores. The Memory of the
world is not a bright, shining crystal, but a
heap of broken fragments, a few fine flashes
of light that break through the darkness. And
so, history is full of tales half-told, and of tunes
that break off in the middle; she gives us snatches

from the lives of men, a peep at some corner of
a battlefield, just enough to make us long for
a fuller vision. All history is full of locked doors,
and of faint glimpses of things that cannot be
reached. The Middle Ages will kick a heel
into the twentieth century, in a Fountains
Abbey—in some straggling ruin—and will ask
us to piece out its former, completed grandeur
for ourselves and to people it with a life of our
own imagining. History can seldom recover
a given set of circumstances and make us see a
definite situation, a particular knot of human
action at a given place and a given time; if two
diplomatists meet in a certain room to settle
a problem, and afterwards describe their pro-
ceedings to their respective governments, or
recall them in memoirs, if Napoleon meets
Metternich in time of crisis at Prague, we can
only recover a dim and faulty account of the
interview from their conflicting descriptions;
and yet this is one of the most precise and clear
situations that a historian might wish to narrate.
And when a Carlyle, in the middle of a rugged
description of the taking of the Bastille, can break
away to apostrophise, in a way that is sublime:

> Oh evening sun of July, how, at this hour, thy beams
> fall slant on reapers amid peaceful woody fields; on old
> women spinning in cottages; on ships far out in the
> silent main....

he is doing something, he is catching the moment, in a way that can seldom be achieved in

history, unless history brings in fiction to help her. History, then, fails the romanticist. Its shortcomings become apparent when we try to particularise, when say, we wish to see a definite picture. About the closest human things, history only tells us enough to set us guessing and wondering.

The history of text-books, the history that can be made out of the recoverable facts of the past, is really little more than a chart to the past. If people think of England there flashes in upon them a panorama, of green fields and telegraph-posts, and intersecting roads and clusters of houses. "England" comes home to us as a jumble of pictures that melt into one another and that we have caught perhaps from the windows of a railway-carriage as we have darted across country. Similarly, if we unlock the past in our minds a score of pictures leap before us, breaking into one another. And the history that history-books can tell us bears a relation to that picture which we make for our-selves of the past, something like the relation which a map of England bears to that mental picture that we form of the English country-side. And just as when we look at an ordnance map we can see where a path runs and can tell where it strikes up hill or down dale, where it touches a wood and where it follows a stream, but if we wish to make a picture of the walk we must put in the hawthorn-hedges, the pretty turns of the path, and the rocky edge of the stream for ourselves—so when we read history, if we wish not merely to see great figures strutting upon a stage, acting a public part, but to fill in the lines of the picture with the robust life of the countryside, and to catch the hundred human touches, if we wish, say, to see the vivid life of three hundred years ago stirring in the crooked streets and topsy-turvy houses that converge upon York Minster, we must charge our history with some of the human things that are irrecoverable, we must reinforce history by our imagination. The public life of great men is before our eyes, some of their private life is open to us; but the life that fills the street with bustle, that makes every corner of a slum a place of wonder and interest, the life that is a sad and gay, weary and thrilling thing in every hillside cottage, is a dim blurred picture in a history. Because of this, history cannot come so near to human hearts and human passions as a good novel can; its very fidelity to facts makes it not perhaps less true to life, but farther away from the heart of things. All the real history of people that a text-book could give is like the chart of Treasure Island—just enough to set a wild heart dreaming; the chart gives generalities, it describes the lie of the land, but if we wish to *see* a picture of Treasure Island we must make the chart the jumping-off board for some play of the imagination.

There is a poem, called "The Old Ships," in which Flecker tells of how he has seen vessels, "with leaden age o'er cargoed," sail "beyond the village which men still call Tyre." These ships, like everything that survives from the past, are a hint to the imagination; they suggest a story; and this is the kind of thinking to which they drive the poet:

"*And all those ships were certainly so old,*
Who knows how oft with squat and noisy gun,
Questing brown slaves or Syrian oranges,
The pirate Genoese
Hell-raked them, till they rolled
Blood, water, fruit and corpses up the hold—

But I have seen...
A drowsy ship of some yet older day;
And, wonder's breath indrawn,
Thought I—who knows—who knows—but in
    that same
(Fished up beyond Aeaea, patched up new
—Stern painted brighter blue—)
That talkative, bald-headed seaman came
(Twelve patient comrades sweating at the oar)
From Troy's doom-crimson shore,
And with great lies about his wooden horse,
Set the crew laughing and forgot his course.

It was so old a ship—who knows, who knows?"

In these lines is shown the lure of all ancient things that store a tale which they cannot tell.

There is a charm and mystery in unremembered things. There is something fine in the
sight of a ridge of hill against the sky when one
does not know what lies beyond or whether
a surprise of rolling sea beneath a sudden fall
of cliff, or a panorama of wooded valleys, is
in store at the summit—so one can only guess
and wonder. And, when, in some border-
village we look at hills that have watched
centuries stride by, and ask ourselves of distant
scenes and old adventure that the hills must
have overlooked, and when we learn that
these matters were writ in water and that about
them not history any more than the stern hill-
crags can break her everlasting silence—then
here is adventure for the imagination, and in
our fancy we play around places that we know
and events that we have heard of, weaving
around "What-has-been" the things that might
have been. We do the kind of thinking that is
needed to turn a map into a picture, the kind of
thinking that might translate last year's National
Budget into a drama of hearts and homes.

It is in this that there lies the first justification of the historical novel, and one way of
giving that particular kind of literature a relation to experience. No infallible generalisation
can give a key to all historical novels and to
everything that appears in them, but here at
least is a useful key that will fit many locks and
will explain much that there is in all these novels,

and moreover will provide a system of relations between these and the history that is a study. It cannot be too strongly stated that the explanation of historical novels is not to be found in the fact that history needs an admixture of fiction to give it spice, to make it exciting, to relieve the boredom. Truth is stranger than fiction and some of the most incredible episodes that have been found in novels have been those which an author has too foolishly taken straight from life. That there is a place for such a thing as the historical novel is due to a certain inadequacy in history itself. History is full of events and issues out of which a story could be made, and of adventures that are exciting enough; it is not wanting in incident, but these things are not stories, they have to be transmuted into story; for there are irrecoverable things in history, and these are the close, intimate personal things, the touches of direct experience that are needed in story-making, the things that we most remember in friends we used to have, what might be called "the human touches." In order to catch these things in the life of the past, and to make a bygone age live again, history must not merely be eked out by fiction, it must not merely be extended by invented episodes; it must be turned into a novel; it must be "put to fiction" as a poem is put to music.

When history tells us that Napoleon did a certain thing, it is the work of each of us, in trying to bring history home to ourselves, to amplify in our imagination what the history-book gives us, and to *see* Napoleon doing the action. It is all very well to be told that a certain event took place, but the past strikes home in our minds with immeasurably greater power if we can see it happening and can catch it as a picture; and this is what we try to do for ourselves when we read a history-book. The important thing is to see the past, and not simply to hear somebody describe it. It is not enough to read of a certain event; we must be there, watching—we must fix it into a picture for ourselves, we must recapture the particular moment. History does not do this for us; just the thing that it cannot do is to catch the moment precisely; so we do this for ourselves; we complete history in our supposition. Every man who has an idea of the woman Mary Queen of Scots, or who can catch glimpses of what happened at Waterloo, has added to history something from his own imagination, and has filled in the lines for himself. The past as it exists for all of us, the world of the past in our minds, is history synthesised by the imagination, and fixed into a picture by something that amounts to fiction. For history fails when a certain situation is to be recovered, or a definite combination of circumstances is to be seized upon, or a particular moment is to be caught. And yet it is a cold and bloodless thing if these things cannot be achieved, and the life of the past is not in any way resurrected without them. The chart must be turned into a picture, if history is to be a recovery of the life of the past and not a mere post-mortem examination. The imagination of the historian does this for him; the most musty of parchments holds for him a story and speaks to a world that exists in his mind; but everybody is not a historian; so historical fiction does the work for all the world; it fuses the past into a picture, and makes it live.

Again, any attempt to recapture the past is limited and inadequate if it keeps a reader conscious of the fact that he is a modern creature, looking at a distant world and comparing it with his own. It is not enough to recover the facts of the lives that men lived long-ago and to trace out the thread of event; we must recover the adventure of their lives; and the whole fun and adventure of their lives, as of ours, hung on the fact that at any given moment they could not see ahead, and did not know what was coming. To the men of 1807 the year 1808 was a mystery and an unexplored tract; they saw a hundred possibilities in it where the modern reader only sees the one thing that actually happened; they never knew what surprise awaited them at the next turn in the road; and therefore, to study the year 1807 remembering all the time what happened in 1808 and in the succeeding trail of years, is to

miss the adventure and the great uncertainties
and the element of gamble in their lives. It is
not enough to know that Napoleon won a certain battle; if history is to come back to us as a
human thing we must see him on the eve of
battle eagerly looking to see which way the
dice will fall, with fears and hesitations perhaps,
with a sense of all the things that may happen
in spite of all his calculations, and with an un-
certainty before all the range of possible things
that may upset his plans. The victory that is
achieved on one day must not be regarded as
being inevitable the night before; and where we
cannot help seeing the certainty of a desired
issue, the men of the time were all suspense, and
full of wonderings. History does not always
give us things like these, for they are irrecoverable personal things; but we know they existed.
They are the things that make life an experience.
And they are the very touches that are needed
to turn history into a story.

These things are what are meant, then, when
it is affirmed that the history that Romanticism
in all of us demands must be at once a picture
and story. And it is in this way that the history-
book which belongs to the "literature of knowledge" is transformed into the "literature of
power."

In the opening chapter of *Ivanhoe* there is a
piece of writing that illustrates the difference
between the historian and the historical novelist

in the use that they make of the same historical
material. In the introductory part of that
chapter Scott recapitulates, "for the information of the general reader," the conditions of
the age with which he is dealing, describing
them in general terms as a historian would.

Four generations (he writes) had not sufficed to
blend the hostile blood of the Normans and Anglo-
Saxons, or to unite, by common language and mutual
interests, two hostile races, one of which still felt the
elation of triumph, while the other groaned under all
the consequences of defeat.... At court and in the castles
of the great nobles, where the pomp and state of a court
was emulated, Norman-French was the only language
employed; in courts of law, the pleading and judgments
were delivered in the same tongue. In short, French
was the language of honour, of chivalry and even of
justice, while the far more manly and expressive Anglo-
Saxon was abandoned to the use of rustics and hinds
who knew no other. Still, however, the necessary inter-
course between the lords of the soil, and those oppressed
inferior beings by whom that soil was cultivated, oc-
casioned the gradual formation of a dialect, compounded
betwixt the French and the Anglo-Saxon, in which they
could render themselves mutually intelligible to each
other; and from this necessity arose by degrees the
structure of our present English language, in which the
speech of the victor and the vanquished have been so
happily blended together; and which has since been so
richly improved by importations from the classical
languages, and from those spoken by the southern
nations of Europe.

This is a history-lesson. A conflict of forces,

a set of tendencies is described in what might be a chapter straight from a history-book. Scott is showing the position that the English language occupied at a given period, and is making the sort of generalisation that it is the historian's business to make. We are not being treated to an essay by Dryasdust; there is imagination in the depiction that is given; but this is the historian's way of treating historical facts; it is essentially the past being described to later ages, it is not the past telling its own tale, giving itself away; and it is a chart to the age rather than a picture. Even in a further sense than this the historian speaks in his peculiar idiom; for he not only describes the world as it was at some time past, but he hauls this world into relationship with the whole of subsequent development and puts it in its place in the whole cinematograph-film that is History. In the concluding sentence he gives the significance of that conflict of languages which he has been describing, and sees it as a link in the whole story of our language. And because of this the reader does not lose himself in the past; he stands aside to compare it with the present. This part of the chapter gives in reality the stage-directions of the novel, and it reminds the reader that he is not in the past, and so breaks the spell.

In the ensuing dialogue, however, where Wamba and Gurth have to contemplate "the

swine being turned Normans," this same historical material is translated into terms of
fiction. It is not stretched, or varnished, or
distorted. The novelist does not try to outdo
history by invention, or to round off the true
historical position by a kind of idealisation; at
least the significance of the chapter does not lie
in any of these things. What is important is
the fact that here the same historical material
is given to the reader in a different way, and is
treated with a different aim. Instead of the
general there is now the particular. Tendencies
that were broadly described before are given
precision, we see what they mean when they
are pinned down to individual cases. Before,
we were given the formula for the age; now we
see the forces that were described manifesting
themselves at a definite place, at a particular
moment. Here the past speaks for itself. We
see it and are in it, we do not simply hear a man
describing it. And instead of that conflict of
languages being put into its context in the
history of language, the novelist puts it into
its context in the whole life of the time, and
hunts out a different set of implications in it.
All this comes with greater vividness to the
reader. History is reinforced by being written
in the story-teller's way.

This is one example taken from a chapter in
which the historian and the historical novelist
chance to rub shoulders with each other, but

the idea is capable of being projected on to a
larger canvas. In the Introduction to *Ivanhoe*
Scott shows how all this can be extended when,
in terms of the historian, he again describes the
set of facts, which he has turned into fiction, the
chart which he has changed into a picture; this
time on a bigger scale, covering the whole range
of the novel.

It seemed to the author that the existence of two
races in the same country, the vanquished distinguished
by their plain, homely, blunt manner, and the free spirit
infused by their ancient institutions and laws; the victors,
by the high spirit of military fame, personal adventure
and whatever could distinguish them as the Flower of
Chivalry might, intermixed with other characters
belonging to the same time and country, interest the
reader by the contrast, if the author should not fail on
his part.

This is a description of a mere relationship
between classes of a society. Scott sees in it a
story. He divines in it just the situations and
issues out of which a story can be made. He
sees its implications in individual lives. Instead
of contemplating its effects on future generations he lays bare its workings in the scheme of
life of people who lived under it. Just as a
prism catches the light and turns it into colours
he stands between the historical generalisation
and his readers and he breaks up the general into
the particular and projects it as a picture. The
result is like the condensing of a cloud into rain-

drops. Fiction is like the dust which creates a sunbeam and helps the sunlight to show that it is there. And in this way Scott does something for history that the historian by himself cannot do, or can seldom do; he recaptures the life of an age, and resurrects a picture of the past.

The historical novelist receives his hint from history, but such examples as these from *Ivanhoe* are enough to make it apparent that this hint need not necessarily be a story ready-made, a sequence of events to be followed. Many historical novels are stories straight from a history-book—the adventures of Guy Fawkes, the sorrows of Mary Queen of Scots—amplified and rounded off by fiction perhaps, and re-told with some variations. History may provide plot and adventure, and fiction may just fill in the lines where history is inadequate or idealise incidents and careers where history is incomplete or disappointing. It is claimed of some of Jokai's novels that, staged as they are in lands where passion and action are intense and full of colour, and drawn as they are from a history that is crowded with romantic and thrilling episodes, they do not need an invention of incident or a perversion of history to make them complete, but are just a vivid re-telling of things that actually happened. The books of Dumas are filled with incidents and situations that are picked straight from history and are marvellously connected into an organised story.

And many writers have assimilated into the body
of their novels incidents that are true to fact
or anecdotes from legend, and so have made
history and fiction fit into each other in dovetail fashion. All this represents one way in
which history can be incorporated into a novel,
but it is not the only way; and the particular
fact that is brought to light by the Introduction
to *Ivanhoe*, as well as by other things, is the
fact that history does not merely inspire fiction
by providing a tale, a thread of incident, a network of action, to be re-told in story-book
fashion; it may only provoke a tale, it may just
provide situations and relationships and problems which give the right kind of issue that is
needed in story-making. Scott saw implicit in
the conditions of the age of Richard I a set of
human relationships which were materials for
a novel. He had the power of divining the
implied story that was hidden beneath a description of Anglo-Norman relations a few
generations after the Conquest.

Everything in life is full of implied story.
Every piece of coal stores up history and a tale
of marvel. Parish accounts that tell of a leap
in the amount of money spent upon "faggots"
in the sixteenth century hold a hidden story of
persecution and martyrdom. There is a tragedy
that can be read into many a newspaper ad-
vertisement, and there are people in the world
who can see the adventure and the wandering

and the panorama that are locked up in a railway-guide. The geography of Africa that might be a dull recapitulation of facts and figures might be turned into narrative, into a story of travels across an unknown continent. And if a politician wishes to bring home to people the consequences of an unwelcome measure he has only to work out a particular instance of hardship that may result from the measure, giving it preciseness and turning it into a story, and he will catch the imagination of electors far sooner than any logic could convince their intellects. It is in this way that the novelist recasts historical material into story-form, and it is in this way that history is made more effectual than the history-book.

Here, then, are the two ways by which history passes into a novel. In the one case it merely gives material that can be woven into story in the same way as a geography-book can be translated into a book of travel; in the other case it provides a story which a writer has to work into his own fictions. The former method is, in a way, organic, since what it prescribes is that a writer shall be true to the life of the past in his inventions; it gives the key in which he must set his tune. According to this, history supplies the metal and the novelist creates the mould. He may invent the characters, the dialogues, the whole range of incident through which it is his aim to make History speak for herself; and he

need not distort the characters of actual historical people to fit them into his story, or do violence
to the chronological table in order to draw
together the threads of his plot. But the second
method implies a further fidelity to the facts of
the history-book and to the sequence of public
events, and it may be called a comparatively
"mechanical" method in that it means that a
story taken from history has to be dovetailed
into the fictions of the novelist; the business is
one of adjustment, and sometimes a wrench has
to be given to history in order to subdue it to
the demands of the novel. And although
seldom or never can a historical novel be found
in which either of these methods is completely
isolated, yet they are two separate things, representing a double set of demands that History
makes upon the writer of novels, and they yield
some fruitful results if they are regarded se-
parately. Wamba and Gurth are representatives
of the one method; and in the same novel
Richard I and Robin Hood stand for the other
method, since their existence implies stories
from history and legend that are required to be
adjusted to the inventions of the novelist.

To say therefore that Scott, in *Ivanhoe*,
translated into terms of fiction the piece of
historical material, the set of human relationships which in his Introduction he described
as being the basis of the novel, is only true in
a general way. But this was the principal thing

that Scott did; and in it he showed his greatest
power, and the historical novel displayed its
finest virtue. In the Introduction to *The
Monastery* he makes a similar confession of the
key-idea of his novel.

> The general plan of the story was, to conjoin two
> characters in that bustling and contentious age, who,
> thrown into situations which gave them different views
> on the subject of the reformation, should, with the same
> sincerity and purity of intention, dedicate themselves,
> the one to the support of the sinking fabric of the Catholic
> Church, the other to the establishment of the reformed
> doctrines. It was supposed that some interesting sub-
> jects for narrative might be derived from opposing two
> such enthusiasts to each other in the path of life, and
> contrasting the real worth of both with their passions
> and prejudices.

Here again is a set of historical conditions
which, even when described in so rough and swift
a fashion, are full of implied story. To turn
these into a novel necessitates no distortion of
great historical events; what the writer does is
to hunt out those situations and problems which
are implicit in the life of the age and in the
described conditions, and which are the kind of
issues that make good story. In the same way
the very title, *The Cloister and the Hearth*, sug-
gesting as it does a collision of loyalties and a
human problem, is a description of something
in mediaeval life that cries out to be turned into
a tale.

The conditions of the life of the present-day, the current habits of thought, the social relationships of men, the economic situation of the country, the welfare of family and Church, and the relations of those institutions and groups that make their conflicting claims upon the loyalty and cover so much of the activity of individuals, are rich with problems and anomalies, and situations and combinations of circumstance which are peculiar to the age, and are the source of most of the issues of the novel of the present-day. The entanglement of the individuals in these conditions produces problems of experience that are peculiarly modern. In the same way every set of circumstances produces its special set of human issues, every age has its own life-problems; and the novel of an age of monasticism will range through a different scheme of problems from that of an age of divorce-law activity, and the world of the Industrial Movement will show life dominated by issues different from those of the age of Chivalry. The twentieth century differs from the twelfth not merely in its language, its dress, its implements and armour, but in its whole experience of life. It is not merely in the suits and trappings that one age contrasts with another; and for this reason the historical novel is justified, as something more than picturesque scene-painting, for it treats of other ages' experiments in living, and depicts human nature breaking in upon a different set of experiences, a different range of problems. When Scott in the Introductions to *Ivanhoe* and to *The Monastery* summarises a state of society therefore, and assumes a given set of human relationships as the basis of a novel, he is carrying with these things the whole range of experiences and issues that are involved in them and that are peculiar to them, and his purpose is to turn these into story as a present-day novelist turns the social conditions of the twentieth century into fiction.

History, then, is not merely a taskmaster to the novelist. Too often the historical novelist has been spoken of as being hampered by history and tied down by chronological tables. He has been regarded as a novelist working under limitations and with one hand tied, history restricting his imagination, and setting him a boundary. But all that has just been said implies that history is not merely the chain that ties the novelist down; rather it is the wing that helps him to soar into a new range of problems and experiences. It is his inspiration, and not simply a tie. When Scott in his Introductions gave himself a basis for his novels it is true that he was accepting certain limitations and agreeing to work within a given set of facts, just as an Arctic explorer agrees to accept the hardships of cold weather; but at the same time he was opening up to himself a different world and a life that rested on a different basis and that so provided him with a host of fresh story-issues.

If the historical novelist regards his duty as being to avoid anachronisms, history will seem to him a chain. The different condition of things existing in the period of which he writes will be a source of labour to him, and a pitfall. But to the true historical novelist they are a glory, they are the whole point of his work, and what was a weakness becomes a strength. If a writer wishes to "work up" a period in order to set a story in it, he will feel history a fetter and every unexpected fact may hamper the story he intended to tell. But if he has steeped his mind in some past age, and has lived in that age, turning it over and over in his imagination, realising the conditions of affairs and the relationships of men and pondering over the implications of these and so recasting the life of the age for himself, then that particular age and those special conditions will suggest their own story, and the historical peculiarities of that age will give point to his novel and will become a power. There is all the difference in the world between a man who has a story to tell and wishes to set it in a past age and to adjust it to the demands of history, and the man who has the past in his head and allows it to come forth in story. There is an immense gulf between the man who works up a period in history in order to tell his story without anachronisms, and a man whose stories come from a mind steeped

in the past. In the one case history has to
be laboriously gathered up around the story,
and it is a burden; in the other case the history
is there to begin with, and the story grows out
of the history. In the true historical novel the
writer has learned to feel at home in the age
with which he is dealing. Such a novel comes
out of a world of the Past that exists in the
writer's mind. The history that it embodies
will be true or inaccurate according as the man
has throughout his life built up that world in
his mind on true foundations, but in any case
that history will come spontaneously; and here
the historical novelist is not a novelist working
under limitations, but one who has captured
new fields of experience and of circumstance
and has conquered a new world for his art.

In all this, too, there can further be worked
out a defence of the historical novel against one
of the charges that are sometimes brought up
against it. The historical novel is specially open
to the temptation of mere picturesqueness. The
one thing that is essentially to be kept in mind
in the whole idea of history that has been
described above, is not that this method of
treating the past is shallow, but that it is specially
liable to descend to shallowness without knowing
it, and to be satisfied with mere externals, and
pageantry, and a veneer of history. Popular
literature is full of empty fiction that sets a conventional story in a picturesque background and
thinks it has done justice to history when it

has clothed its personages in coloured costumes
and given their language a touch of the obsolete,
and raised up a stage-setting of courts and
camps and Gothic architecture; and the draw-
back to the historical novel lies in the fact that
the touch of strangeness, the sense of the far-
away, the hint of colour and romance in all
these, too often makes the emptiness of the
show more tolerable; the fine feathers disguise
the worthlessness of the bird below. But if it
is remembered that every state of society has
its peculiar experience of life, that every age of
history shows mankind breaking in upon experience and upon the problems of life at
different points, and that each generation has
its attitude to existence, and its peculiar synthesis, then it must be seen that the charge of
shallowness is not one that can be made against
the whole idea of historical novels, and that these,
like any other novel, may be rich with experience
and may touch human issues. A story that
describes a Roman watching the decay of the
Empire that he had been taught would endure
for ever, and seeing a surging barbarian life
flood into its borders like some awful eruption
of Nature before which human effort is futile
and men can only look helplessly on, may be a
mere melodrama, unredeemed by its pageantry
and picturesqueness; but it can be more—the
story of a unique experience, and of one of the
urgent moments in the life of mankind. Shallow-

ness is not the evil of the historical novel—it is only its danger.

Lastly, it may be said that the inspiration of the historical novel is not merely history, but also geography. To a person for whom history did not exist at all a landscape would be merely a flat picture; to one who can think history into it, it has a dimension in time. To some people the ruins of Rome may be a poor heap of fragments, pieces of broken art-ware; but to Gibbon and Gregorovius who brought to the place a sense of the history behind, those ruins were the starting-point of a trail that led back to the glories of ancient Rome and were the clue to a story. If people re-tread the scenes of a distant childhood it is not merely a flat picture that comes before their eyes, but other scenes behind it, scenes that the memory has stored and that are somehow locked up in the present one; the very landscape looks different, and is richer because it breathes the past. To an architect a building is not merely a dead weight of stone, but a mass of forces striking in different directions and brought somehow to a poise; the whole structure is thrilled with life and in every line of it there is motion. To a historical mind similarly, a building must *look* different. It has not merely length and breadth and height, but also a certain "throughness," an extension in time; behind the "Now" of that building there is a long trail of Moments of the same building, the place has not merely a few associations with the past but a whole context in history; and the sight of the walls at the present time is only the last picture of a cinematograph-reel which represents all the hundred Yesterdays that are folded up within the stone. Our fleeting "Now" is only the last term of an ever-lengthening series. Time is locked up within scenery and buildings; and the aim of history is to unlock it and to make it speak its secret.

What we call historic sites and buildings represent places in which this secret has in some measure been recovered. They have not existed longer than other places in geography, but they are places about which History can remember things. The cinematograph-film which represents their extension in time is not completely locked away from us; and the historical mind means among other things the power to feel the film there and to recall pictures in it at the mere sight of the place, on the mere suggestion of geography.

In Sir Walter Scott this power of reading history into places existed in real intensity.

To me (he said) the wandering over the field of Bannockburn was the source of more exquisite pleasure than gazing upon the celebrated landscape from the battlement of Stirling Castle. I do not by any means infer that I was dead to the feeling of picturesque scenery—but show me an old castle in a field of battle and I was at home at once....

If he saw a scene about which tradition or the history-book had nothing to tell, he still saw the history there, and tried to read the past into the place. Someone wrote of him:

> He was but half-satisfied with the most beautiful scenery when he could not connect it with some local legend, and when I was forced sometimes to confess with the knife-grinder "Story! God bless you! I have none to tell, sir," he would laugh and say "then let us make one—nothing so easy as to make a tradition."

Such a story invented around a place, such an attempt to call up history out of a scene, is really an act of homage, an offering made to the place, a work of dedication.

History is rooted in geography, and the historical novel, which is a novel that seeks to be rooted in some ways in actuality, finds one of its roots in geography. The quotation made above from Scott's Introduction to *The Monastery* is part of an explanation which the author gives of the reason why he chose the celebrated ruins of Melrose as the scene of his story, although he described the place as "possessing less of romantic beauty than some other scenes in Scotland." Of Jokai it has been said "The world around him—Hungary, Russia, and Turkey—breathed more romance and imagination than did the Highlands to Scott or France to Dumas"; and here was the inspiration of the writer.

Historical novels are born of romanticism of a kind; but they are a romancing around objects and places; they have a basis in reality, and their roots in the soil. In this way there is

something more firm about them than is found
in the more vague and dreamy products of
romanticism—those dim romances of some
undefined no-time, no-place, which have a
"stained-glass window" vision of a mediaeval
past and lack the link with earth, and can only
be connected with the historical novel in the
way a fairy-story can, that is by the remote
suggestion of the past that is contained in the
airy words "Once upon a time."

And if in the historical novel there is devotion to locality and a feeling for the history that
breathes through the soil, all this comes out
large and most complete where geography and
tradition, love of place and pride in its heritage
of story, combine in patriotism. Patriotism that
so often rings false is in this true, in that it
becomes the consciousness of belonging to a
place and a tradition. Even where it seems
most local and confined, even where it contains
no sounding of the trumpets of nationalism,
and where its author holds no patriotic motive,
the historical novel cannot help reminding men
of their heritage in the soil. It is often born of
a kind of patriotism; it can scarcely avoid always
being the inspiration of it. In this way it becomes itself a power in history, an impulse to
fine feeling, and a source of more of the action
and heroism which it describes. The historical
novel itself becomes a maker of history.

II

I T has been noticed that the ostensible theme of *The Cloister and the Hearth* is an instance of a human problem that came out in a particular form in mediaeval life, but exists in some form in every society. The problem is one of loyalties that cut across each other and pull different ways. A modern novelist would be likely to treat this as a study in human experience and would analyse the disruption it would cause in the individual soul. Reade, however, is a Victorian, who lived before the psychological novel had become the fashion, and he does the Victorian thing; instead of treating this problem as the real theme of his novel, he pushes it on one side, and makes it simply the excuse for sending his hero on a journey, so that his story becomes very largely a story of travel.

The simplest kind of novel is the novel of this kind, which gives a string of happenings that befell the hero in his wandering through the world. It is not the working-out of a plot, or the following-up of a situation. It does not turn upon a definite set of relations which provide a problem for the novelist to solve, a knot for him to untie; it does not hunt down a given set of circumstances to some logical issue. It is simply a chain of happenings, an accumulation of incident; one episode does not grow out of another, each leading to something deeper; but events merely succeed one another at various turns in the road which the hero has to travel, and the only connection between them is that they all happen to the same person. Dickens is an example of this kind of novelist, who takes any excuse for sending his hero on his travels, and narrates the various things that turn up on the journey. The *Pickwick Papers* belong to this class, for they do not represent a scheme of action working to a certain issue, but are a chain of episodes that never lead to anything and might continue for ever. In the adventures of Pickwick, therefore, Dickens is really describing a world in which his hero is wandering; just as in *David Copperfield* he is not so much revealing a character as painting the world that his hero passed through in his life's journey. Such novels are really tales of travel; the world of the story is not merely the background for the hero, the setting for the story; rather the hero is the excuse for describing the world. Sometimes that world is a topsy-turvy place, like the one that bewildered Pickwick, or the fantastic "Wonderland" that Alice found herself in; sometimes it is a Lilliput, or some imagined future state of things, or it may even be modern society. In a historical novel it will be some past age, described as a far-country.

The simplest form of treatment that can be given to history in the novel is that of the story in which the hero travels a bygone age, and the reader follows him as into a new world and peeps over his shoulder to see what he sees. The age, the whole scheme of things as it then existed, is described in the adventures of the wanderer and at its point of contact with an individual life. This happens to some extent in every historical novel. Apart from any conscious description of the background of his story the novelist must always be betraying the peculiar conditions of a particular century, since the fate and fortunes of the actors in his drama are the result of their entanglement in the affairs of the time and in the system of things of the particular moment. But in a work like *The Cloister and the Hearth* all this is raised into a method and is the way adopted for making history betray itself; the wanderings of the hero make the book pre-eminently a descriptive one, and the fact that the novel is rather a chain of incident than the working out of a particular process of action, makes the world of the story more important than the plot. The hardships of Gerard at strange inns, his illnesses, the brawls in the countryside, the companions whom he meets, and the steps in his career are simply the means by which the age manifests its character, and in them history is speaking. There can be no simpler example than this of the translation of history into story.

In so far as this method of treating the past is followed in *The Cloister and the Hearth* or in any novel, it means that an age is regarded as a set of conditions, a system of things, that is looked upon as static and is described at its points of contact with an individual life set in it and, so to speak, entangled in its network. That individual may be the creation of the novelist and his chain of adventures may be pure invention. His life is a candle that lights up corners of his age as it is brought into them, and the places at which he touches his age and runs up against the characteristic circumstances of his time, his points of contact with the machinery of society, may be ideally chosen to show up the character of his time. His life may then sum up his age in a way in which no actual individual life that is ever lived can in itself sum up the peculiar conditions of the age in which it is set. In *The Cloister and the Hearth*, at any rate, a century is fixed for us as a picture, as a static thing. The cinematograph-film of history is stopped there, and one particular photograph on the reel is projected into the book.

All this, however, is elaborated when the set of conditions to be described is regarded not as a static thing, but as dynamic. *Barnaby Rudge*, by reason of its very faults, perhaps more than by virtue of any greatness, is an example well calculated to illustrate this point.

The first section of this book is a love-story very largely conventional. It is not a piece from a historical novel at all; the slight references to history and the picturesqueness of background

and costume are not in themselves sufficient
to give this story of homely private life the
character of historical fiction. Nothing that
happens is calculated to make a particular age
of the past betray itself; there is no chord that
awakens a response from History. Nothing but
the slight element of colour and picturesqueness
exists to prevent this from being a story of any
century; and at the most there is only the
suggestion of an indefinable Past such as is so
attractive to the shallow romantic novelist.

In the middle of the book, however, as if by
an afterthought the reader is introduced to that
uprising of the people which is known as the
Gordon Riots. In the fervour of describing the
riotous mass-movement Dickens seems to forget
his original plot and to lose sight of his principal
characters. The story loses itself in a vivid sketch
of the Gordon Riots, and the original problems
of the book are only solved in a perfunctory
way at the close. The reader who has made
himself interested in the homely affairs of the
Willets and Vardons is irritated to find that
these are pushed on one side, and that the whole
novel takes a swerve in a different direction.

And yet the bareness of the historical setting
of the first section of the book, and the lack of
all suggestion of a political background or of
any complication of individual issues by larger
political events, sets out in more effective contrast the later theme of the novel, that irresistible

sweep of a great mob-action rushing like a
blight over any corner of life that lies in its
path. If the Gordon Riots come like a flood
into *Barnaby Rudge*, playing havoc with the
fortunes of the story and swallowing up everything they meet, it is what they do in real life.
If the reader loses sight of the men and women
in whose fate he has become interested, and if
all that he can catch is an occasional glimpse of
them, lost or helpless in a crowded surging
stream of life, it is what would have happened
to them if the flood had carried them away in
actual existence. The very faults of *Barnaby
Rudge* as a piece of construction, its irritating
weaknesses as a story, are calculated to in-
tensify the effect that a historian of some popular
upheaval must always try to obtain—the effect
of a sweeping, ravaging flood that surges over
the peaceful lives of individuals and swallows up
men and their homes and their little aims and
concerns, and leaves a devastated track behind.

A similar treatment of a historic movement
occurs in *A Tale of Two Cities*; but in this case,
precisely because Dickens kept a closer hold
upon his story and fixed his eyes more steadily
upon his principal characters and his main
issues—precisely because he did not lose himself
in the setting of his novel, in the "world" of
his story—the same cataclysmic result is not so
apparent, the tremendous sweep of the destroying
storm is not so graphically reproduced. The

story is less irritating because we do not lose sight of the characters whose fate is the theme of the novel, but the Revolution does not come so powerfully as a devastating wave and at the same time it does not come with the awful precipitancy of the Gordon Riots in *Barnaby Rudge*, but it is anticipated and prepared for in advance. Still, even here, the historical idea that stands out is the spectacle of a movement of the people that is overwhelming in the havoc that it plays with the individual lives and concerns caught within its orbit.

In these instances the set of conditions in which the individual is involved are not static, but dynamic; and the character of them, and the sweep of them, come out at their points of contact with individual lives, and are revealed in the way they touch the concerns of men and break in upon the personal fortunes of a few people. In these instances, therefore, the wind is described by its effect on the feather that drifts helplessly in it, and we follow the flood by keeping our eyes on some particular object floating in it and swept forward by it. All this would be sufficient to make a historical novel and to justify it; for such a novel would in a way outstrip the history-book in the telling of history, since it would not merely describe a distant past to us, but would take us into it; it would not be a telescope as history is, enabling us to see something far away, but would be a

bridge leading us over the gulf that divides past
and present, and so annihilating time. In such
a novel we should see the past from the point
of view of the past, and recapture an age as it
comes to individuals in it; we should be not
merely twentieth-century spectators watching a
distant scene, but would become contemporary
with the past, and having an inside knowledge
of it. In all this the historical novel would
challenge the history-book in its own fields.

But this does not span the full range of this
kind of novel; it omits something that historical
novelists almost always go out of their way to
achieve. Here the incidents and adventure of
the novel may be purely fictitious, and the
characters may be inventions; and only the
world in which they are placed, the currents
that sweep over their lives, and the movements
that overwhelm them need to be real; the novel
is true to the life of the past, and is faithful to
the age with which it is concerned, regarding
the age as a set of conditions to be conformed
with. It is true to the spirit of the age; and may
describe the past as a far-country; but it may
have nothing to do with the actual events of
the past, and with history regarded as a chain
of story. Every happening that it relates may
be an invention; and it can do all that has just
been claimed for it without containing any
specific incident that ever took place. It may
tell its history by revealing history in its workings

in an imaginary life set in it; in the same way
as a teacher may illustrate the force of gravity
to children by talking about its workings on an
imaginary apple. It may be in a way true to
history without being true to fact.

If a story is told us about some spot with
which we are acquainted, then, although the
story may not be true, it touches us somewhere,
it has a root in actuality and so makes us listen,
in a way which would be impossible if the story
were told, so to speak, in the air. If we hear
some anecdote that is narrated about a friend
of ours it holds us even if we know it is a legend,
in a way which it could not do if it had not
fastened itself upon something real. If a story
can plant one foot in actuality then it belongs no
more to the clouds, and it gains an added power
from having established a connection with
reality. It is this kind of additional effectiveness
that historical novelists seek to obtain. They are
not satisfied that the world of their story shall
be true to the world of the past, and that situations and incident shall grow out of that world.
Their novel is not merely background, but
story, and to them history is not merely the
world as it once was, but also a quarry of incident. And once a novel is regarded as a story,
and incidents or episodes are looked upon as
the important thing, the units in it, the things
into which the chapters arrange themselves—
then a historical novel is still "in the air," and

is only historical in a vague and unconvincing way, and lacks one of the strongest roots in actuality, if its events are fictitious and its characters imaginary, so that nothing in the story ever really "happened." There is a great difference between the novel that simply lights up the history of an age, and illustrates the conditions of the time, and one which is itself a piece of historical narrative. It is when the reader can feel that the things that are being related actually took place, and that the man about whom the stories are being told really lived although the stories about him may not all be true; it is when the thread of incident in the novel, as well as what might be called the texture of the book, can in some way be called "historical," that the work is most effective in its grip on actuality. And if this is true, an author looking at the life of the past and at the things that happened in history is like the artist looking upon a scene in nature and "longing to do something with it," longing to turn it into something and to recreate it, in such a way as to express himself as well as to reproduce actuality.

In *A Tale of Two Cities*, then, Dickens was content to describe the grim fires of the French Revolution not directly, but in the reflection that they threw upon a few imaginary individuals; the events that were "historical" in the sense of being memorable, the public events that held

the stage at the time, he was content to portray
in their effects upon the homely lives of one or
two fictitious characters. But there is a more
direct and pointed way of transferring things
from history into the novel, and this method,
when superimposed upon the other, gives a
story an added link with actuality. In any novel
adventures and incidents, exploits, intrigues,
and fine action rich with character may not
merely be good fiction, but coming direct from
history may be like the cords which bound
Gulliver in Lilliput, each of them a tie holding
the novel to earth, and fixing it in reality. To
people for whom incident is an important thing
in the novel the historical value of *The Cloister
and the Hearth* lies not so much in the picture
that it gives of an age of the past, as in the
foundation that its story can claim to possess
in the life of the Father of Erasmus. In *Barnaby
Rudge* it is the description of Lord George
Gordon and his circle that gives the novel a
tangible connection with history; the story becomes a story about somebody we know, a
person we have met before; history provides
the writer not merely with the world of his story,
but with actual story itself. It is regarded not
merely as a picture of things as they once were,
but as a store of narrative and of anecdote too.

History often gives the novelist the hint
for story, since the conditions and circumstances of an age are full of implied story, and

are enough to set anybody tale-telling. In a larger and more direct way, as will be shown, it may further provide a theme for a novelist; in the lives of people like Mary Queen of Scots, or Richard I, and in affairs like the Gunpowder Plot or the Jacobite risings, it may give not exactly a story to the novelist, but a fit subject for novel-study, something to work upon, a problem to develop and solve; for not only on their public side, but still more on their personal side these things invite story; and history itself supplies a number of incidents about them and a general outline of broad events which set the key for a novel and fix the lines within which the novelist will work. But beyond all these there is a mass of human experience, and a wide circle of life, a whole World of People—and all these, just the things that the novelist must most trouble himself about—concerning which history, as has been shown, can tell only an inadequate story. The novelist who deals with kings perhaps, but more often with ordinary fighters and citizens—with courts and parliaments sometimes, but more often with hearts and homes, looks to history for "things that really happened," regarding history as a storehouse of narrative, and finds there only episodes. Things only come out of the darkness on brief occasions, and many things are only hinted at, and many threads of story are carried a short way and then broken and dropped; History

bursts out here and there in a few fine flashes
of story; but very rarely is there a consecutive
flow of narrative such as would make a true,
but coherent and continuous story for a novel—
a long connected strand of story-issues only
waiting to be re-told in fiction. This history
that is narrative comes in fragments, in mere
snatches, to be incorporated in fiction. The
novelist who seeks to tell "things that really
happened" must clutch at episodes. It remains
to be seen what use he can make of them.

All novelists seem at times to introduce into
their works situations and happenings straight
from life, or founded upon fact; sometimes things
that have been accounted incredible or un-
natural in novels, have been defended by
authors as having been copied straight from
nature. No critic, however, would seriously
admit that the appreciation of any novel is at
all influenced by a fact like this. The literal
truth of an incident is not sufficient justification
for its inclusion in a novel, and does not even
make its presence in the work more valuable;
still less does it affect the worth of the whole
novel as a faithful representation of truth. It is
clear that the same reasoning must apply to
historical episodes incorporated into fiction. The
mere inclusion of some actual happening in a
story, the attempt to drag in a piece of history
and to patch it into a novel, is not justified by
the addition of a footnote informing the reader

that "This incident actually took place." The fact may interest a reader, but it is a separate kind of interest that it gives, and it does not affect the total appreciation of the novel as a complete unity. The occasional and arbitrary use of happenings from history, the sending of a few pistol-shots of actual episode into a piece of work, does not alter the character of the whole, and does not give the novel one foot in reality, a root in actual life, any more than Dickens's use of events from real life brought his novels into closer touch with reality and with truth.

Yet there is an important use that can be made of historical incident in fiction, and a more effective way of transferring anecdotes and events from history into the novel. This time the author does not exactly put his finger upon some particular period in history, and work upon that, using the conditions of the time as the hint for story; and does not apply himself specially to a certain wave of popular movement or fix his attention upon particular historical characters; these things he can never ignore, but here they are not his first thought, and it is not around these that his work takes shape; his unit is rather "the thing that actually happened"; his eye is upon the incident, and he works upon that; and the result appears in the existence of a peculiar type of episodical novel, which consists of pieces of story, isolated episodes, loosely strung together upon a thread of fiction, not worked into one another and fused together by fiction; and succeeding one another in such a detached way that sometimes the unity of the whole is very far to seek. The entire novel tends to split up into particular knots of story, one cluster of narrative having perhaps only the most accidental of connections with another, and each being in a way complete in itself.

This kind of novel can only come from a history rich with the right kind of episodes. It would seem that there are certain periods in the world's story, and in this case the Renaissance would be assuredly one, and there are certain countries and localities like the Hungary that Jokai depicted and the Highlands of Scotland, which are peculiarly favourable to this method of treating history in fiction, since they appear to throw out their history in the form of episodes that ask to be turned into story. When life is adventurous and full of colour and crowded with striking incident, when, against a romantic background, there is the assertion of vigorous personality, resulting in novel turns of action, and exciting combinations of circumstance; and, above all, when these are the kind of things that are remembered in story and tradition and song, so that history is a store of incidents, and a tale of exploits and intrigues and adventures rather than a mere narrative of social development and public events, then the *raconteur* must find this history

a treasure-store of materials for a historical
novel that shall be a succession of brilliant
episodes rather than the working-out of some
great theme, some large process. The by-ways
of history, too, the dusty corners of the past,
away from the main course of broad political
movement and public event, are lit up by out-
of-the-way incidents and stories that the history
of history-books misses in its wide sweep; and
these, although rooted in fact, are things that
a story-teller would love to have invented, and
they ask to be re-told in fiction. This, then, is the
field of the novel of historical episodes. In
faults as well as in virtues many of the books of
Jokai are striking illustrations of the form; but
many novelists have adopted it with some variations; and even a book like Merejkowski's
Forerunner, in spite of its unity in the character
of Leonardo and in the spirit of Renaissance, is
only an example of this way of treating episodes;
it may work them into a finer whole, and centralise
the interest of the reader, and send one great
idea throbbing through each; but it can scarcely
avoid taking shape before the eyes of the reader
as a series of fine flashes of incident, each in a
way self-contained, and finding their connection
more in the fabrications of the novelist than in
the fabric of real history.

The first book of *The Forerunner* is a key to
this whole method of abstracting episodes from
history and setting them into a novel; especially

as it is one of the places where an author not only
tells his story, but at the head of his chapter
reveals his authority for it in contemporary
writings, and so allows us to see just what was
his "hint from history" and what use he made
of it. This incident of the "White She-Devil"
is a self-contained episode, one of the stray
stories that history can tell. The novelist fills
in the lines of the brief historical narrative. He
does for it what an illustrator does for any author
—he adds detail and colour and gives preciseness and a certain elaboration to the general
outline, the vaguer description, that is given
him to work upon. More than this, fiction
somehow amplifies the whole bearings of the
event, and enlarges its significance, making it
almost symbolic; and further provides links,
that a reader can identify and put his finger
upon, slight links, just the necessary connections
that bring the affair into its place in the whole
book, and so form the excuse for its presence
in the novel at all. But the most noticeable thing
of all is not merely the episodic nature of the
material that is taken from history to be incorporated in fiction but the episodic treatment
that is given to it. The stage is set for this
particular incident, and when it is completed
the curtain falls and we are carried away to a
totally different scene. A wealth of historical
detail is grouped around this one episode; the
episode is the thing that the whole section of the

book clusters around. When this anecdote has been worked into a picture the author takes up an entirely new canvas, and starts over again for the next, raising up a fresh historic background for it. In this way one thing succeeds another like slides displacing one another in a lantern, a shutter separating each; things do not run into one another with the connectedness of a film. If the episodic novel reaches a unity at all, its episodes are generally related to one another as facets of a diamond, rather than as links in a chain; the spectator changes his ground, his point of vision in passing from one to another; he does not slide unconsciously from one episode to the next.

In a complete and organised type of novel, episodes usher in one another and grow out of one another, luring the reader to a prepared climax, each carrying the architecture of the whole a step further, and all conspiring to produce an event to which the whole novel is tending. Such a novel comes to the reader as a process unfolding itself, a theme being worked out. In the looser type of fiction that *The Cloister and the Hearth* represents, things follow one another in a chain, and find their unity in the fact that they all happen to the same person; so that the novel shapes itself round the hero, rather than into a theme. But in the episodical novel it is not any unifying theme that is the nucleus of the story, nor is it any particular

character, but it is the "episode." Each chapter
is in a way a fresh inspiration and has its source
in an isolated historical fact. History supplies
not so much a run of narrative for the whole
novel, as unrelated episodes which fiction may
fasten together, but which stand alone in their
original historical setting. The whole method of
taking narrative itself straight from the history-
book, in spite of its pointedness in reproducing
definite incidents that actually happened, has
its limitations in the fragmentary nature of
history itself, or, at least, of the history that
deals with the personal human things of story-
interest. That history can only reach to episodes
as a general rule, so it is in danger of producing
something that is not a novel at all but a series
of imaginative excursions into the past, a collection of historical "sketches." The conflict of
loyalties in historical fiction is seen here. A
historical novel can not be made up of history
that is picked out in snatches, and of this alone.
A collection of episodes is disjointed narrative.
It may be fused into running story by the
imagination and the inventions of an author;
or it may still remain in broken narrative, yet
find a different unity in a novel that is something
more than a narration. But in either event
fiction must help out history.

*   *   *   *

The achievement of Dumas is sufficient to
show what can be done in a novel that is above

all things a narrative. Dumas did not merely
set his novels in history and weave his stories
around men who actually lived; he took actual
situations and events, incident and action from
history; and his greatness lies in the fact that
he did not reproduce these in a broken episodic
fashion, putting each in its own frame, and on a
separate canvas, he did not merely patch them
into fictions of his own and sprinkle them in his
works, but he worked them in with his imagined
episodes into a thread of running story.

He was lucky in the field of his labours. The
history of the France that he described flashes
out in brilliant episodes, and is rich in characters
and situations that give the hint for more. It
is the history of the great—of kings and statesmen and of the first in the land—but it
is at the same time an extraordinarily personal
kind of history, not a tale of dry public events.
It was set in scenes of gallantry and colour, and
was just distant enough to come to readers with
a glamour. And Dumas by the multiplicity of
the characters whose fortunes he intertwined
in his novels laid a wide field of its incident and
adventure open to himself, and brought a large
range of actual recorded facts into the scope of
his novels.

But it was his way of twining history and
fiction into one another, instead of tacking the
one on to the other, and of making one story
out of them, that gave him his power. He ran
the whole into one flowing narrative. A list

could be made of the incidents in his novels
that are taken from history but only a close
student, and a man as learned in the history of
those times as Dumas himself, can detect the
joint, the place where the actual and the invented episodes fit into one another. History
and fiction cannot be disentangled in these
novels, and a separate rôle, a particular function
in the combined work, be assigned to each; they
grow into each other, and reinforce one another;
each somehow gives its character to the other;
so much in the novels is actual history that this
lends its character to the whole, and gives it a
root in actuality, so that the works come as a
narrative of France, a stream of national story,
a kind of history themselves.

The works of Dumas, therefore, do not come
as a series of shifting episodes that displace one
another. There is no stopping to set the scene
for an episode or an event. The story will run
into the Massacre of St Bartholomew and
straight out of it, and there will be no drawing
of the curtain, no break in the action, while a
stage is being arranged. Exploits and adventures and intrigues come in quick succession,
and keep the reader on tip-toe. The result is
an effect of sheer movement. Everything seems
in motion. The novels are pure story, and
Dumas is pre-eminently a teller of stories.

History may be regarded as a chain of ages
that overlap, and run into each other and then
fold under—as an ocean of human life, genera-

tions of peoples, coming in waves through the
centuries. It may also be regarded as a thread
of narrative, a stream of story, winding through
time. Dumas more than anybody else has
succeeded in turning history into narrative like
this. His works are a thread of story running
through centuries of the history of France.

They are not pictures of France. Dumas's
eye does not sweep the broad landscape of
France, does not see the whole of it. The deep
sound of the ocean of peoples does not rever-
berate through his books. The great life of
France is not in them, like a sounding-board
against the noisy events of court and camp. The
ebb and flow of popular movements does not
surge through them; and only occasionally is
the swelling tide of some big heave of human
effort let in, to hint at the mass-life of France
outside the pages of the story. Dumas does not
stop to paint a horizontal scene of France as
a whole; and because of this his thread of story
keeps moving, but there are no broad landscapes
of history. There are courts and state-rooms,
hunting-fields and street-scenes; but these do
not echo the sounds from mountains and plains
and the larger France. Dumas gives a trickle
of narrative running through history; not a
surging flood. He deals with the men who in
their day were the men who mattered, the life
which, while it was being lived, was considered
to be the life that counted in France; and he

deals with the region which stood out in high light above the dark masses in the past, and about which, therefore, history could remember things.

* * * *

The limit of the things that history can remember must determine the range of most historical novels, and fix their choice of subject. It is useful to see the bearings upon this of that slight differentiation in meaning between the words "historic" and "historical." A "historical" event is anything that really happened in history, but a "historic" one is a celebrated one —one that would not be forgotten and that made a noise in the world. A "historic" character is a famous character, very often a public man. And so history comes to mean, not the world living out its centuries, but the stage upon which the big things happened and were noticed, and upon which far-reaching issues were worked out. In all the ages of the past there have been a few people who have moved the world, and have cut a great figure in their day, and behind these there has been the mass of people who did not lead, but followed, who did not act, but watched, who were the material upon which the great men worked, the instrument upon which the men in high station played. They were spectators of the historic event, as much as we; but only the actors in it belong to remembered history. History then becomes, as

it were, the limelight directed upon the arena
of loud-sounding events and brilliant action,
leaving the whole theatre of spectators in darkness. It is the platform for Cromwell and Caesar
and Napoleon and Milton; captains and kings
and discoverers and heroes feel at home upon
it; but behind it are the people who watch and
suffer and serve these Cromwells and Caesars;
they leave no memorial; and only occasionally
at moments of intense history-making, do they
break through on to the platform, and sweep
across the stage, and show that they are there.

This arena of great "historic" event provides
a more spacious theme for the novelist than
mere episodes abstracted from universal history
can do. Instead of wandering in the interesting
by-ways of the past, and finding surprises of
thrilling episode in out-of-the-way corners, the
novelist may boldly face the full course of
important events, and plunge into the fate and
fortunes of the great. The historical novel then
becomes an embodiment of historic things in the
sense of far-reaching, loud-sounding issues, and
it has a wider canvas, an ampler scope. Here it
is not incidents merely that are taken from history, but a whole block of action and happening,
a whole act from the mighty drama of the ages.
History provides not merely snatches of tune
that have to be worked into some sort of connection with one another, but a whole orchestral
theme, which the novelist re-organises and works

out afresh. It gives a set of issues that are
capable of novel-study, and are full of human-
meaning, and embody a problem in experience.
Only, it must be said, all this is limited, or at
least its character is determined, by the fact that
this theme must concern men who have been
in the public eye, and events that have been
enacted in the sight of the world and so have
been registered on the memory of the world. And
a novel that deals with public events and national
affairs and treats of people who are remembered
in history because of their part in the political
movements of their time, presents a problem
that is peculiar in one respect.

The theme of a novel is human experience
and the fate of human beings in the world. It
covers all the things that the heart has ever
touched, all the varied harmonies that it has
happened to strike as it has brushed against life.
It may concern itself with the big events that
send their echo through the ages, it may feel
the great heart that pulses in the life of a whole
continent, it may tell of movements that have
broken upon the world and changed the fate of
peoples; but its supreme interest is in a mere
man. In a sense it is true that every man is alone
in the world, and feels himself stranded amongst
"everything else." He is, and he cannot help
being, the centre of the circle of his own horizon;
he must see his fellow-creatures as part of the
"everything else," part of the world against

which he stands out; and that outer world must come to him as an experience and an adventure. The one thing that exists for him is this experience of the world.

And that is the one thing that exists in him for the novelist. It is the aim of the novelist to stand by the individual and feel life with him. The waves of some political or historic movement may touch the man and so come within the range of the novel, but they will not affect the man any more than his own special, homely concerns—probably they will only affect him through those little concerns. It is his own hopes and ambitions and fears as he finds himself set up against the world of men and things, his conflict with circumstances, his moods and his glad moments, his risks, his falling in love, his bewilderments, his relations with men, that make up a novel. Some writers, like Jokai and Dumas and Stevenson, will be specially concerned with the adventure of his life; the things that happened, the things he undertook, the surprises and the thrills; these are the story-tellers whose novels are narrations; but others, and especially the modern novelists, look more to the experience, and regard it as a theme to be studied as well as a story to be related. Perhaps these are the true historians, for they record experience, and it is they who in the most intimate and personal way capture life into the pages of a book.

The scope of the novel, however, is not limited to the life and affairs of ordinary people, average humanity. There are people who have felt life more intensely than others, and have reached loftier heights of experience than most. Things may have come to them with greater power than to the mass of people. Perhaps life is for ever a bigger thing because they have lived and have swept new ranges of experience, and have happened upon new chords, fresh harmonies of feeling, and have in some way communicated these to the world. Then again, there are men who, not because of any intrinsic greatness of mind or heart, but by reason of what we mortals can only regard as the incalculable thing, and can only call "chance," have been placed in exceptional circumstances and situations of novelty, and so have struck upon new elements of experience, or fresh life-problems. In the careers of such men life seems to come out in new forms, and in unexpected ways. If they can be captured for the novel, then the novel can range over the finest regions of life, and can communicate their experience to the world, and so enlarge life for everybody else.

It might seem that these, the men of exceptional powers, and the men who find themselves in unusual situations, are the very people whom history does not forget; but this is only true with one great limitation. They must be people whom exceptional powers or the apparent accident of circumstances once brought into the public eye. They must be "historic" people, as well as "historical," if our knowledge of them is to be more than fragmentary. If a man is memorable in his public life, then the world will see to it that his private life does not go unrecorded and unremembered; the personal things, the experience of the man even, will become known in so far as they are not specially concealed and in so far as such things in the life of an individual are communicable to others. The novelist who can do justice to these is widening the range of the novel, and bringing new and intenser experience into the kingdom of the novel, and is exploring life in its most intractable regions. He reaches life as it has been lived, at some of its finest points, and at some of its most splendid or most pressing moments. History, it has been seen, may give wing to the novel, and may expand its range. What is true for the life of an age or a people is here true also of the life of individuals. Biography also may place new fields of experience within the scope of a novel.

Statesmen and kings and scientists, then, are not shut out of the novel, but the novelist's interest in them is not an interest in the statesmanship, or in the rule, or in the science but in the whole personality of the man behind these, and his theme is still a human heart caught into the world and entangled in time and circumstance. The politician, the economist, the philosopher and the psychologist are all students of mankind in a way, and can claim that their studies are human studies; but they only start with human nature, and they soon run into theorems and formulas and lose themselves in their own categories, and so are swept away from contact with flesh and blood. But the novelist does not begin with men and then leap into abstractions. He keeps his hand on a human pulse all the time. Political issues coming into his work are put into their whole context in life and experience, and instead of being abstracted into a realm of political science they are fastened to men and women who are "political animals," but are something more as well. The novelist sees the whole of life, and he goes one further, and one better than the scientific historian in that men are to him (as they are to themselves) ends in themselves, not merely servants of a process which consumes them, not merely means to an end and links in the chain of history. A man may lose himself in politics or mathematics but to the novelist it is still the man that matters.

The things that are far-reaching and historic are not to him more important than the things that are momentary yet external. He would give more to catch a real glimpse of Mary Queen of Scots tapping her foot in a moment of im-

patience than to possess a logical statement of
her political position at any time. He will not
ignore the politics of some Prime Minister of
a former century, but he would love still more
to surprise him at play. A great political speech
might come within the scope of his work, but
where a historian might be tempted to sum up
the whole event in terms of politics, he would
notice too the headache that made the statesman
depressed and the heat of the building that made
him irritable, the private worries that he could
not throw off and that tormented his mind and
perverted his judgment, and the sight of a man
sitting opposite whom he detested in private life
and who wore an annoying tie. The novelist
would attempt to recapture the moment, rather
than to estimate its historic significance, and the
things which he would notice would be those
which influenced the man at the moment,
though they did not always concern the politics.

There was once a day when kingdoms were
a piece of family property that could be sold,
and the whole politics of a land depended on
marriages, and wars raged for years over some
intricate point in a genealogical table; in those
days public events were part of the private
concern of a king, and as surely as the succession
to a throne depended upon family inheritance,
the affairs of the kingdom depended upon personal whims and private ambitions. There was
a time when the religious system of England

had to be changed because a king wished to marry a lady about his court. In the world that Dumas described so well, personal prowess and individual exploits determined events, and private concerns and the prejudices and feuds of families cut across the larger history of a nation. There have been times when a slight offered to a king's mistress has been more tragic in its results than a lost battle or a lost election; and who knows how much the history of a reign has been affected by an influence like that which Buckingham had upon Charles I, or the Duchess of Marlborough upon Queen Anne? In all these things private life complicates even where it does not determine public events, and all history is full of imaginable situations like these that invite novel-treatment. When personality counts in public affairs, and many things, other than purely political motives— even things which seem trivial and accidental —determine the conduct of a man at any time, then the mood of a moment, the personal discomfort or family irritation that might have caused it, the perversities of whim and arbitrary desire, and a hundred other things in a man may affect history. The historical novel, not consciously perhaps, but still demonstrably stands for this fact. It emphasises the influence of personal things in history, it regards man's life as a whole and runs his private action and his public conduct into each other, as it ought to do; and it turns the whole into a study of human nature. Even when dealing with an action that seems purely political it will root the action in personality, not merely in politics. Because every public action that was ever taken can be regarded as the private act, the personal decision of somebody, historic events can become materials for the novel, in spite of the fact that public affairs and political matters are not in themselves issues for a novel.

The novelist looking at a historic figure sees personality where the scientific historian is tempted to see only the incarnation of a policy. He feels flesh and blood where the ordinary history-reader complains that he is given only abstractions. Every historic decision that comes under his review has for him a context in the mind of the man who made it and not simply in the politics of the day. Behind every great name he sees a human being, with a peculiar experience of life; even if history does not tell of the experience he knows it is there, he thinks it into history and endows the man with it, and he completes the personality in his imagination, bringing in fiction to supply what history fails to give. That is true resurrection, that is the reason why historical novels are full of life and of people, where history is often bloodless and dead.

It is evident from all this that there are particular periods and particular problems in

history that are specially adapted to this kind
of novel-treatment. An age of riotous indi-
vidualism and of aggressive personalities is more
suited to it than one in which corporate action
determines events. An age in which war is a
game, an orgy of fun and fine fighting, is better
than one in which war is an intricate and organised science. A king who governs by whim
is more fitting than a politician who is merely
the mouthpiece of a party, the servant of
organised action. More and more as life
increases in complexity and the world becomes
organised on impersonal lines, the historical
novel that treats of the action of personalities in
history and the interaction of private life and
public events, must find its course intricate and
hard. Ultimately personality counts to-day as
much as ever it did in history; it is still the real
power, but its influence is not direct, and immediate, and palpable; things perhaps can be
traced back to the influence of individuals, but
it is an ultimate influence, an influence in the
last resort, and it does not show itself on the
surface of life. It is fairly true to say that the
historical novel, where it deals with politics and
public events, must seize upon those periods
of history and those phases of life in which
personality not only matters in the last resort,
but makes an immediate impression and stamps
itself directly upon the world. The mental
struggle of Charles I before he consented to

sacrifice Strafford to his enemies, and the personal influence which immediately contributed
to his decision are a theme for the novel; but
it would need a large admixture of fiction and
a wilful exaggeration of the interaction of
private concerns with political issues, and a
perversion of history to treat a modern change
of ministry in the same fashion.

Nothing could be more suited to this idea
of the historical novel than a reign like that of
Mary Queen of Scots, in which the whims of
a woman are a national concern, a direct and
immediate influence upon historic events, and
history for a time hangs upon her moods and
prejudices, and her very love-stories have a
kind of political significance.

Such is the sort of theme that a novelist can
take from history—one in which public affairs
appear as somebody's private concern, and so
can be treated in a personal way. A set of historic events or the career of some historic figure
is placed in its context in personal experience,
and is worked into a novel that may be a study
as well as a story. Somebody has said that every
individual carries within him at least one novel,
the story of his own wrestle with life. It may
be added that every historic theme, every chapter
taken out of the past contains within itself not
merely a story, but several stories, all of them
equally true, all of them representing the same
set of events as they came to the various people

concerned and struck home in different ways—
all of them facets of the same truth.

What Browning did in *The Ring and the Book*
for the record of a "sordid police case" historical novelists, taken all together, may be said to
do for history. Browning took his ground-work
of incident and related it nine different times,
each time from the point of view of different
people concerned, and he showed that a tale
re-told from a different standpoint and around
a fresh person is really a new tale. The whole
world of the story shifts round when a new point
of vision is adopted, the same set of events come
differently and with a different bearing. To
relate a narrative from the point of view of the
criminal in it, and then from the point of view
of the victim and then from that of the hero
is not merely to tell the same story in different
ways; it is something more striking than that,
it is to give a new tale every time. Events that
are joy to one person are grief to another, perhaps; one man's glad story may be somebody
else's sad story, and if the centre of sympathy
has been changed everything in a narrative
must take a fresh shape around it. Nothing can
better illustrate the richness of history and the
many-sidedness of life than this fact; and the
historical novelist represents it in his treatment
of the past. He may make a story out of the life
of Mary Queen of Scots, and out of the same set
of facts he may make a totally different story,

told from the point of view of Bothwell or Elizabeth. He may enrich history by bringing out its many-sided implications, and bringing to light the variety and complexity of the significance of historic happenings.

But it is a bold thing and a tremendous venture, to write of the intimate thoughts and experiences of the great, and even to guess at the motives of their actions. Carlyle said that only a great man could even recognise a great man. If this is the case, many must be tempted to ask, How can the novelist pretend to do more than this, and to understand a great man, even to re-create him in all his greatness? How can he make the statesman statesmanlike, and the queen queenly, and the prophet passionate and soul-stirring? To do this the novelist must within his own mind sweep the range of experience not merely of the ordinary man, not merely of the literary man—these things he might be expected to do—but also of the mighty forgers of history and the pioneers in experience; and he who very likely cannot understand the moods and caprices of his own landlady and who has never pierced the mystery of personality as it exists in her, must record the intimate thoughts, the slightest wave of a mood that passes over the mind like the wind over the grass, the half-conscious motives and the deep solemn experience in people like Mary Queen of Scots or Oliver Cromwell or Richard I who were in a

way geniuses in living, and in particular phases
of life and experience. If the novelist does not
do this adequately, if his statesmen are not at
least statesmanlike even though not true to
facts, if his kings are not at least royal in some
way, if he does not give great men the touch of
greatness and the soul of grandeur, his characters are merely pompous puppets, in fine dress
and on high pedestals, a piece of show, a
mocking pageantry.

Perhaps the most impressive way of bringing
great men into the historical novel, is not the
method which makes their lives and careers the
central theme of the book at all, demanding
intimate treatment, and close appreciation and
analysis. Many historical novels are stories of
ordinary everyday issues in the lives of people,
and deal with some personal concerns of fictitious
characters, and with the things that make up the
ordinary kind of novel; but these novels become
"historical" ones by the fact that their drama is
played out as it were in the shadow of great
public events. Some well-known, historic
character looms in the background, larger
historical issues cast their shadow at times and
perhaps at some point the narrow concerns of
the individuals whose fate makes up the story,
cross the path of these, and become interlocked
for a moment with some piece of history. In
Woodstock for example the homely problems of
a few fictitious characters, and the small vicissi-

tudes of a locality occupy the centre of the stage.
Their story grows out of a set of historical
relations as it existed in the days of the Protectorate, and is a story born of the conditions of
the time in the way Scott suggested in the
Introductions to *Ivanhoe* and *The Monastery*.
The first chapter of the book brings out history
in the form of story, it is a peep at England in
the days of the Protectorate, it is a "sample," a
kind of specimen picture of the age and the story
is implied in the conditions of the time. There
is a suggestion of the awful omnipotence of
Cromwell, and a feeling that the distant sternness of his rule is coming near and will soon
be brought home to people, but the Protector
himself is a solemn figure in the background.
There is a kind of impressiveness in the way the
story actually crosses his path. The reader is
ushered into the presence of the great man, and
Cromwell is not treated familiarly—we do not
pry into his mind and we do not see through the
man, but everything is as though in an impressive
moment in real life we had once met the man
and felt him greater and more distant than ever.
When Charles II comes into the book a similar
thing happens; we peep at a corner of his life,
we catch one side of him, but the whole man is
not laid bare, and we know that there is a world
within him that is not revealed. In this way the
feeling that to ordinary citizens of the country
there is something impenetrable in these great

people is maintained. Life to all of us is a chain of private aims and personal concerns and family or homely issues that seem to be all the world to us as they come one after another; but far above we can feel that larger historic issues are being worked out oblivious of our petty concerns, and ignoring our little lives. Only at times do our paths cross. A war or a popular movement at some time may touch the family and even break up homes, sweeping away the issues and affairs that were our little world, but even this only accentuates our feeling that over our heads, as it were, a great history-making is always going on; and in the days when personalities like Cromwell moved the world directly, and held an immediate sway over events, such men must have come to the minds of ordinary human beings as distant peaks come to the traveller, as objects of solitary impenetrable grandeur and of awful power. In describing the world like this, the kind of historical novel of which *Woodstock* is only one of a whole variety of examples, depicts life in a relevant and significant fashion.

       *   *   *   *

In all these ways history can be translated into fiction and can gain something in the process; but above them all there towers a form of novel that is more sweeping in its treatment of history, more ambitious in its interpretation of life, more bold in its way of looking at the world.

In it the novel reaches beyond itself, so that to call it any longer a "novel" is to give it an inadequate title. It is a prose epic; but because it is a way by which history is turned into fiction it cannot pass unnoticed.

History has been taken to mean the world looking back upon itself, and remembering things. But after memory comes experience and the reflection upon experience. In our individual lives we are not content to recall things that happened, we do not just have memories, and stop there; but we relate these to one another, and see meaning in them and work them into experiences, through which we come to see life as unity and as purpose and as a process. In a similar way there comes a time when history must be something more than reminiscence, something more than memories of this age and that age, of one happening and another happening, of a man here and a man there; it must be something more even than a chain, a succession of these; it must be a web, a unity, woven of them all. It must be the experience of Man on this earth, face to face with Nature, warring with the elements, and lonely under the sky—man at grips with Life through all the ages. It must be a symphony, each orchestral part doing something to express the great idea of the whole, and each moment, each year, each age adding a new bar to the score, and carrying the architecture of the whole a little further. History is not merely the story of men and of their deeds and adventures; it is the Epic of Man.

If the past is looked at in this way the individual ceases to be the centre of focus. Men and women and their lives become fragments in the whole trend of things, mere ripples on the surface of a great world-life. The surge of historic movement, the pulse of life underneath all lives becomes the real theme of story; though this can only manifest itself, can only become tangible in individual lives. The artist who tries to capture the wind into a picture or into words knows what this means. He may show the leaves scattered by the wind, and the trees bent before it, and the countryside devastated by a hurricane; but all this is not wind. He may paint a ship in full sail before a breeze, or an ocean whipped to fury; but these are not the wind; he may describe the delightful play of the wind in your hair, or the trail of its fingers in the grass—but that weird mysterious thing, the wind, that comes in whispers through the trees and sounds an organ-tone deep and tremendous as an ocean as it sweeps over the heather, eludes him every time. It can only be described in its results. And the same is true in history. The epic in historical fiction describes the tangible and the particular, and the concrete; but it suggests a living principle behind these, working in these, and only manifesting itself in them. The epic writer looking at the life of the past sees an accumulation of events, of details, of instances, but in them all he divines a synthesis, and sees one throb of the great heart of the world; and behind them all he feels one life-principle working itself out and carrying men with it as a tide carries the foam or as the Spring brings the buds.

The power and awfulness of the wind are not to be recognised by a glance at the weather-vane or at the thistle-down floating through the air; it is the cumulative effect of a hundred different details, a hundred different things touched and changed by the wind, that makes the wind seem beyond escape; it is the suggestion of the broad spaces and unlimited stretches through which the wind can range, that must give the impression that it is everywhere; and it is the gentleness of its touch here, and the crash of its irresistible rush there, that must give the idea of its powerful yet subtle activities. The epic that seeks to describe the heart that beats as one behind the life of a whole people must point to the pulse throbbing in a hundred places. It is the overpowering effect of accumulated detail and of all this spread over a wide canvas, that must conspire to show some surge of a deep-sounding tide in the lives of people, some breath that sweeps through the life of a race; it is only in this way that the ubiquity, the power beyond escape, the hundred varied ways of working, of

some life-principle behind the affairs of individuals, can be brought out. The historical
novel that is an epic, is, then, a mighty production, a great conception minutely worked
out, a piece of architecture. It is the novel
carried to a higher power. Its hero is not a
man but a force in men. Its vision of the past
is one of titanic powers working underground.
It grapples with Destiny and dares to look the
universe in the face; and it spells out Fate and
strikes at the stars.

The love of wide canvases burdened with
significant detail; the large vision of the past as
one in texture with the present and as a sublime
urge of humanity rising above obstacles and
fighting its chains; and the poet's power of
synthesis, made Victor Hugo the great master
of this epic romance, as he was its conscious
exponent. Nothing could better illustrate his
sense of the one-ness of history and the sublime
tragedy of Man's experience in the world than
his introduction to *The Toilers of the Sea*:

Religion, Society and Nature; these are the three
struggles of mankind. These three struggles are at the
same time his three needs; it is necessary for him to have
a faith, hence the temple; it is necessary for him to
create, hence the city; it is necessary for him to live,
hence the plough and the ship. But these three solutions
comprise three conflicts. The mysterious difficulty of
life springs from all the three.

Man strives with obstacles under the form of super-

stition, under the form of prejudice, and under the form
of the elements. A triple fatality weighs upon us—the
fatality of dogmas, the fatality of laws, the fatality of
matter. In *Notre Dame* the author has denounced the
first; in *Les Misérables* he has described the second; in
this book he points out the third.

With these three fatalities that envelop mankind
is mingled the inward fatality—the highest fatality—
the human heart.

This quotation alone is sufficient to show that
the conception of the Epic of Man rests, not
upon the idea that the past is a new world for
the novelist to range in, but on a fact that is
equally true from its own point of view—the
fact of the one-ness of experience and the unity
of the past with the present. The historical
novel that is a universal epic, therefore comes to
men as an interpretation of Man's experience
in the world. It is cosmic in conception. Also
it is the work of a man who is not merely
novelist, but poet; for though experience is all
one piece, it comes to us in fragments and we
only know it in parts, and the man who wishes
to understand it and to map out its meaning,
must in looking at past and present find a
one-ness that is not apparent in that mass of
details and people and events that confront him;
he must divine a synthesis. This seems to be
the conscious aim of Hugo, and there is a
tremendous power in his achievement that is
not to be found in the interpretation of large

history that Merejkowski seeks to give in his trilogy. In such works as these history as well as the novel is carried beyond itself, and raised to a higher power.

The national epic is not so broad in its sweep, not so consciously an interpretation of universal experience as what might be called the Epic of Man. Here again it is not an individual that is the hero of the story, but something that might almost be personified, a force working in the lives of men; only, in this case, the stage of the drama is the Nation at some tremendous moment in its history. The quiver through a whole people of some breath of national feeling is described like the stir of the wind upon a pool; the throb of a whole nation in some intense crisis is caught into story. And as this surge of feeling in a people becomes most apparent at the point at which it meets resistance, no theme is better for this kind of novel than that which describes in a people the bitter sense of national liberty thwarted, and of national aspirations refused, the growing consciousness of repression and an increasing desire to resist the oppressor. Where these exist love of liberty comes as a yearning and an aspiration and a vision; fine impulses become conscious because they strike against an obstacle; and they become aggressive since they feel themselves thwarted. Nothing makes a more powerful motive for a novel.

This epic of national liberty is often itself inspired by the national aspirations it describes. Perhaps it would be too much to identify it with the historical novelists of Eastern Europe, especially since Hugo's *Ninety-Three*, the hero of which has been described as being the Revolution, is admitted to be one of the best examples of it; but it seems fairly true to identify it chiefly with those countries in which the sense of national aspirations being thwarted has recently existed and has been an impulse to art and literature, and a good many of the historical novels of Eastern European writers are distinguished by the throb of national feeling that strikes through them. And this kind of novel is specially calculated to produce the precise feeling that it describes, to stir readers to the aspirations which are its theme, and to be a force for liberty itself. Such a result is even aimed at by writers, so that the novel becomes in danger of developing into a novel with a purpose.

Victor Hugo's *Ninety-Three* is a striking example of the epic of national freedom; and it illustrates much of the mind of its author and much of the character of this type of novel. It has been said that its hero is not a particular personage in the story, but rather the Revolution itself. Hugo had the powerful grasp of the character of large and complex masses of detail, the genius for synthesis, the eagle-like sweep of an imagination that can comprehend a multi-

tude of things and combine them in one principle
—the very things that were needed to make a
gigantic movement of the masses the theme of
an epic. In his descriptions of the Vendée there
is a chapter on "the spirit of the place" which
shows his way of thinking; he demonstrates in
fine flights of comprehensive statement that
"the configuration of the soil decides many of
man's actions and the earth is more his accom-
plice than people believe...," and he describes
the difference that exists between the mountain
insurgent like the Swiss, and the forest insurgent
like the Vendean: "The one almost always fights
for an ideal, the other for a prejudice. The one
soars, the other crawls. The one combats for
humanity, the other for solitude. The one
desires liberty, the other wishes isolation. The
one defends the commune, the other the parish.
...The one has to deal with precipices, the other
with quagmires...." The voice of Hugo is in
all this, and whether it is true or false it shows
a mind that jumps to synthesis. There is much
more of the same kind of generalising in this
book, *Ninety-Three*, and often Hugo seems to be
preaching when he turns aside to throw out
some incidental flashes of it. He sees not only
the trees but the contour of the land, the character of the forest; he grasps not merely maddening
events and a confusion of men bustling with
action, but divines the whole curve of the mass-
movement. He can speak of "the immense

profile of the French Revolution," thrown across
"the deep and distant Heavens, against a background at once serene and tragic." It is significant enough that he can think of the Revolution as something like that.

Those chapters of the novel, however, which
describe "the streets of Paris at that time," the
conversation between Robespierre, Danton, and
Marat, and the Convention itself, and the
Vendée, are weighed down by an accumulation
of significant and often grim detail, a piling-up
of incident upon incident, and example upon
example. In these the Revolution is not only
shown as having a character, a profile, but also
is revealed as being a living thing, a vivid many-
sided creature, betraying its character in a host
of unexpected ways, flashing out in a thousand
fresh surprises, in a multiplicity of manifestations. It is shown to be like Nature that sends
out a crocus here, a daffodil there, green buds
and almond blossom somewhere else, and the
song of the birds everywhere, all of them saying
in a number of ways that the Spring has come.
It comes to us like the wind that moves the
grass and the weather-vane, the smoke and the
sailing-ship and the creaking door—and in a
score of different voices makes itself heard to
men. The mass of detail reveals the Revolution
as an intricate thing, a complex tangle perhaps,
but most of all as a vivid many-sided life, a unity
in a hundred variations, a principle that is for

ever finding a host of new ways of expressing itself.

Hugo described the Convention by heaping up a store of details, and burdening his whole chapter with a weight of concrete instances. Each of these was significant in itself and showed the Revolution in some way leaping out and leaving its mark in history; and the cumulative effect of the whole revealed the bewildering variety of the processes and the life of the Revolution. Before he closed the description, however, he wrote a few paragraphs that reveal the key-idea of the whole. He had been speaking of the men of the Convention, he had already turned aside to tell us that the Convention "had a life," and he had piled up a host of instances of how that life had broken through into incident and action, and had mentioned the turbulent spirits that made up the life of the Assembly.

Spirits which were a prey of the wind (he continued). But this was a miracle-working wind. To be a member of the Convention was to be a wave of the ocean. This was true even of the greatest there. The force of impulsion came from on high. There was a Will in the Convention which was that of all and yet not that of any one person. This Will was an Idea, indomitable and immeasurable, which swept from the summit of Heaven into darkness below. We call this Revolution. When that idea passed it beat down one, and raised up another; it scattered this man into foam and dashed that one upon the reefs. This Idea knew whither it was going, and drove the whirlpool before it. To ascribe the Revolution to men is to ascribe the tide to the waves....

The Revolution is a form of the eternal phenomenon which presses upon us from every quarter, and which we call Necessity.

This, then, is the idea that gives a synthesis to all the mass of details, this is the wind which reveals itself in the multitude of spirits which it moves. In this kind of thinking Hugo is trying to interpret man's experience upon earth. His story is more than a narration. He has seen the epic in history.

Above all this, however, the French Revolution comes to us as the hero of the novel because of the remarkable way in which it is personified in the man Cimourdain, who seems to have caught something of its life into himself. "He saw the Revolution loom into life," says Hugo; "He was not a man to be afraid of that giant; far from it. This sudden growth in everything had revivified himself.... From year to year he saw events gain in grandeur and he increased with them." The year 1793 represents above all things the time when the "something" inexorable in the very idea of the Revolution became most marked, most pressing, and Hugo has made this the prominent feature in his characterisation of the year. The book is full of cruel alternatives, and of Councils and men torn between unreserved devotion to the Ideal, the Revolution, and generous impulses towards men, humanitarian feelings. Cimourdain is the personification of this struggle between utter selfless service to a cause and a heart's loyalty to a friend. Hugo's whole characterisation of him hangs upon this feature of his character, this cleavage in his soul. The theme of the whole novel is the life and conduct of men like Lantenac and Gauvain as they are brought face to face with the inexorable demands of their Cause. Lantenac, however, is a Vendean; and Gauvain at the supreme trial sacrifices the Cause to his feelings of generosity. Cimourdain alone is immovable, and is devoted to his Ideal to the point of being inhuman. He personifies the Revolution, therefore. He is more than a man, he is greater than a hero of a novel, he is the central figure of an epic.

III

Molly was a handsome fool....She lacked the historic
sense; and if she thought of Rome at all, supposed it
a collocation of warehouses, jetties, and a church or
two—an unfamiliar Wapping upon a river with a long
name.

Maurice Hewlett's heroine had known only
Wapping and Wapping was her world. She
could not think of Rome as being, so to speak,
the blossom of another sort of tree—a place
where the very sky looked different; but she
must take Wapping as the pattern of things.
Her untravelled mind could not see that Life
as it strikes through the Earth, crystallising into
towns and cities and breaking out in buildings
and fashions and thoughts, is one thing here
and another thing there, and ever finds fresh
forms for its expression like an artist in his
moods. Molly could not dream that all history
—and, behind history, geography—had con-
spired to make Rome a different picture, a
different mood, from the Wapping she had
known. She "lacked the historic sense." It was
not that the warehouses of Rome might be
different from those of Wapping, or its churches
bigger, or all these set out in an unfamiliar way;
it would have been wrong if it had been possible

to think of Rome as an unfamiliar Wapping, without warehouses, jetties and churches, all. The truth was that Rome was one poem, and Wapping was another poem; and each was the clothing of a Life. Each was a personality; in a way, a world in itself. Each had that sort of one-ness and identity which gave it an "atmosphere" of its own.

For a mind that is moulded to a locality the historical novel can come as travel and as an opening of the windows of the world. It is not a history-lesson, a book that sits to facts, a record of things as they actually happened; or rather, it may be all this and it has an added power if it is, but its appeal and purpose are not here. When a reader comes to the historical novel he is not, or ought not to be, ignorant of the fact that it is a form of fiction that he is reading, and that history in it is mixed with inventions in a proportion which he cannot be expected to estimate with any precision. The novel does not replace the history-book; it is a splendid thing if it drives us to the history-book, if it provides us with something—some sort of texture—in which the facts of the history-book, when we come to them, can find a context and a lively significance and a field that gives them play. The real justification of the novel as a way of dealing with the past, is that it brings home to readers the fact that there is such a thing as a world of the past to tell tales about—

an arena of vivid and momentous life, in which men and women were flesh and blood, their sorrows and hopes and adventures real as ours, and their moment as precious as our moment. The power of the novel is that it can give to people the feeling for history, the consciousness that this world is an old world that can tell many stories of lost years, the sense that the present age is the last of a trail of centuries. It makes history a kind of extension of our personal experience, and not merely an addition to the sum of our knowledge.

For the novelist therefore it is more important to depict the past as a world different from our own, and to show something of its character and colouring than to map out a particular path in that world and to track down a particular course of public events. It is more important for him to breathe the spirit of a bygone age, and make his book the stuff of its mind, and recapture its turns of thought, its fund of feeling, and all its waywardnesses than to chronicle events with precision and keep tight to big political happenings. The supreme thing for him is to catch the age as a synthesis, to reproduce its way of looking at the world, its acceptance of life, and the peculiar quality of its experience, rather than to relate things that actually happened. Looking to some distant time he does not, so to speak, see "notes," and relations of notes, but catches a "tune"; he figures it, not as a heap of facts

and happenings but as the World-life in one of
its moods. He enumerates, describes, com-
ments, perhaps; but the real secret of his art is
that in doing all these things he disengages a
subtle influence—does it as if by stealth—he
breathes a thing that quickens and that is as
spirit to the body; so that while he is describing
or reflecting or narrating the age itself seems to
conspire with him, and presents itself in its
"atmosphere."

Atmosphere eludes the analyst. It might
almost be said that to define it would be to
explain it away. Probably the novelist most
successful in producing it would be unable to
describe how the thing is done. It is part of its
essence that you should not see its working; if
you detect scaffolding anywhere there is dis-
illusionment and you are back to earth again;
if you discover the spell it revenges itself upon
you and sulks, and though you may admire the
cleverness of it, it is magic no longer for you.
It likes you to forget it, and captures you unawares, and then you will recall how it was
atmosphere that stole you; but hunt it, and you
thwart it, and put yourself out of tune for it.
You may remember that some book was a
world, and that world showed itself in its
atmosphere, and the atmosphere was everywhere, but you cannot put your finger upon a
printed page and say "it is here." In this it is
worthy of its name, it defies immediate appre-

hension. It will not meet you in the face. It is a conspiracy.

Various ages of history have their atmosphere —the Middle Ages, the Renaissance, the eighteenth century; but atmosphere does not move in step with history, does not belong merely to epochs. Countries and localities have it—like the Highlands of Scotland, or Hungary; and the atmosphere of Puritan London is not that of the contemporary Paris. The peasantry of Scott and the racy story-world in which Dumas was himself, come to us with their atmosphere; and a monastery or a diplomatic circle or the court of some king may carry theirs in a similar way. These are definite areas that cover the lives of men, and they have not merely characteristics but characters of their own. They are not simply modifications of one another any more than Rome is Wapping with a difference. Each is a fresh canvas and in calling them to mind we mix our colours and our emotions differently every time; each leaps in turn as a whole into our minds, so that we think of them as being not merely varied groupings of notes, but different tunes altogether. Each, like a personality, has its particular way of looking at the world and its peculiar attitude to things, and this comes out in a particular twist of mind in men, peculiar tricks of thought and prejudices and shades of feeling. The peasantry of Scotland must have

a different sort of jokes, a different range of
allusions from the courtiers of Louis XIV.
Various of these regions of life and circles of
activity must have their special phraseology,
even a kind of dialect of their own. Atmosphere
belongs to a region that is a life, an identity,
a world in itself, and a peculiar synthesis; and
he who has the atmosphere must have found—
or rather felt—the synthesis.

These various areas of life—ages of history,
localities and circles of activity—may be viewed
as being worlds in themselves and as having
a life of their own; but that life only shows itself
in its results, as for instance, in the prejudices
and turns of thought and habits and peculiarities of speech of the members who make up the
world. And just as a child learning to read at
first spells out only letters, and consciously
combines them into words and only gradually
learns to see words as a whole and take them in
at a glance—just as a learner in music at first
only sees notes and has to use some effort in
order to combine them into a chord, and only
later comes to grasp a chord at sight—so the
student of history at first sees only these isolated
details and pieces of fact, and must gradually
come to the point at which his mind can jump
to a synthesis and see the one life that is the
source of a variety of facts. The novelist
consciously reproducing facts from history,
copying its handwriting letter by letter, ad-

vancing by accumulation, and straining for a faithful presentation of details in the life of a people, can scarcely avoid betraying the mechanism with which he works; but the writer who has caught the principle that lies behind all these facts, and sees not merely men and actions and sayings, but a life underneath all these, has caught history at its source; he can throw down his scaffolding. Step by step he has followed facts and weighed his evidence and hung upon details, until there has flashed in upon him the something that gives light and meaning to them all, and changes them into a vision. The age of history is no longer to him a sum of information, but a world that has been won and appropriated. More facts and details that he may amass find their setting and significance, find a context in that world; they may also check, or change, or amplify his acceptance and appreciation of it; but to him, that age of history is a world in his mind, like a childhood's scene half-remembered, and he may withdraw to it at will, retreading it in his thinking—crossing and recrossing, and playing upon it in his imagination, all the time recasting it in the process.

Behind a thousand sunsets there lies a world where men were full of the hunt and the anxious harvest-times, and slept with their swords near at hand. To them the Atlantic Ocean was a thing to raise terror, a place for strange story-telling; the demons were not yet driven from the woods; and earth was a precarious place in which the elemental forces seemed inexorable. It was a world of wild mythologies, and of simple things half-understood. It comes to us —we "remember" it—in fragments like this; and we try to piece it together again. The centuries have tiptoed and gone, and the things that people have been afraid of, the things that have raised a thrill, the things men have talked and joked and told easy lies about, have not always remained the same. Their logic has been different from our logic, as a schoolboy's is different from a priest's. The things which in their thinking they were always referring to, mirrored the world they knew. The ideas that were handy to their minds, the words that came soonest to their lips, the turn that was easiest to their talk, their whole fund of metaphors and expressions, betrayed their preoccupations and lit up the background of their lives. Perhaps the Sunday church-bell sounded differently to their ears and reached a hidden corner in their minds. Perhaps they had not learned to think of the stars as loveliness. For them there could be no evening silhouettes of chimney-pots and telegraph-wires against the glaring moon, no dream of long white roads that should shake with hurried, humming traffic—the pictures they felt at home with were not the same as ours. And just as, in a land where earthquakes are to be expected, the fact must give a twist to the art of building, the thoughts of architects, so, in those distant ages, the world that people knew, the things they felt at home with, a hundred significant details, moulded the forms of their thoughts, and conditioned the terms of their thinking, and made the maps of their minds. It is by entering into this fact that the novelist can do more than simply copy some recorded details of their world, and can recapture something of their life. In so far as he succeeds at all it is because the things which conditioned their thinking, he accepts for himself. He does not analyse them from the outside, but submits and surrenders to them, makes them in fact his own. Telling a tale of some far-off world, he will not speak of the stars with the love of the poet; he will remember that the astrologers had made them a dread relentless destiny, so that this would be an alien fact. He will explore things of this kind, and take them into his thinking, and make them part of his kingdom; for it is a surprise of facts such as this—which show the age true to itself in an unexpected way —and it is the cumulative effect of a host of them, that powerfully make for atmosphere.

And just as he enters into the things that conditioned the thinking of these men of former days, the novelist in a larger way fits life to the things which conditioned their experience, and moves within the framework of the age. It is the same human nature all the time, which he is describing, but it comes in different disguises, and is always finding fresh symbols for itself, fresh forms for its expression. The same essential fact, the same inner experience, takes different turns in its unfolding. The boy who runs away to escape the drudgery near at hand may be the same in every century; but to-day it will be the dullness of school-routine that brings unrest and the cinema that brings incitement; while in some bygone age it would be the cruelty of apprentice-life that became unbearable, and tales of high adventure on the Spanish Main that made the world inviting. This would lead to a different wayfaring. It is a fresh story altogether. Love may be ever the same but it will not blossom out into the identical facts, it will not raise the same issues, it will not lure to the same adventures, altogether it will not unfold its story in the same way, in various worlds of convention. The novelist who knows the experience must weave it to the pattern and run it into the mould of the century with which he is dealing, he must fit it to the machinery of life as it then was, he must translate it into the terms of the age. Present experience, in so far as it is eternal experience, can be referred back to a different world, where even to the farthest detail of its working it will run into different forms; and the facility, the inevitability with which this is done, so that you do not find a modern love-story transplanted into alien soil, patched into

an old tapestry, set in a mere background of
mediaeval staging and dress, but the whole
theme overhauled with insistent reference to
the conditioning features of the age, by a mind
that has not wearied of playing upon the implications of these things—is one of the things
which make the age as reproduced in the novel
come to us with conviction, and with atmosphere.
Perhaps the lack of this constant way of running
back to the past in thinking till everything has
been remoulded is what makes *The Cloister and
the Hearth* fail in atmosphere, and seem like a
story of modern convention merely clothed in
an old-world dress and staged in mediaeval
setting, without coming as a live blossoming of
mediaeval life.

It is recalled in Henry James's *Notes on
Novelists* how Robert Louis Stevenson made
Edinburgh his "own."

And this (we are told) even in spite of continual
absence—in virtue of a constant imaginative reference
and an intense intellectual possession.

In a similar way if at all—the historian wins
over for himself, and comes to possess an age
of the past; but whereas Stevenson in his
absence could constantly shoot back in his mind
to a distant, remembered Edinburgh, in the
case of the historian it is in a peculiar sense an
irrecoverable, and so to speak, only half-remembered world that is "referred" to, and the

man cannot go direct to the original to confirm
the mental picture he retains. He can never
know the past just as Stevenson knew the city
he had actually trodden, and there is more of
himself, more of the personal element, in his
appropriation of it—how much, he cannot tell,
because he can never go behind his vision of the
past to compare it with the reality. We who
may hold some place as Stevenson did Edinburgh, and perhaps remember it as a distant
thing we knew in the old days, and retread it in
our imagination and refer to it in our thinking
—we can return to the spot itself to verify the
impression it has left in our minds and see if
our picture is true; and returning we may be
shocked to find how Memory has played us
false, how the Edinburgh that was in our
thoughts is out of touch with the real thing.
Working with an equally imperfect "Memory"
the historian cannot do this, cannot put back
the clock to a distant age to see if the "world"
he has created out of it in his mind has parted
from reality. And yet, given that "world" of the
past as he holds it, it is still true that he makes
it peculiarly his own, in that he constantly
traverses it in his imagination, it is as a magnet
to his mind, he carries present things back into
it and is for ever making calls upon it, till it
becomes a part of his thinking. It was because
Scott had worked like this upon the history that
he knew so well, and because he had entered

into the past in this special way and made it a country of his mind, that Hutton could write of him that "He had something like a personal experience of several centuries."

The man who does this and can feel at home in a certain "world" of history, who saturates himself with the spirit of an age and breathes its very air, and having touched the life of a time has turned it over in his mind and has played upon it and pondered over it in his thinking— will learn to catch unawares the turns of thought that were current then, will reproduce in a spontaneous way the habits and modes of life of the past—the things he would otherwise have had to copy with servility—and will enter without effort into the very tricks of speech of some former day. Instead of transplanting facts and specific details direct from the history-book into the story-book, he will find expression for the life which he has made his own, letting it blossom out into its own appropriate "facts," its inevitable manifestations. Atmosphere, though not merely the result of spontaneity, any more than the electricity is the result of the wire, demands this as its necessary concomitant, as electricity demands the completed circuit. Perhaps it may be said that atmosphere is the result of a conspiracy of details that come in an effort-less way from a mind that has entered into the experience and made appropriation of the "world," of some age in history. It belongs to the past age in some sense; but it cannot be separated from the personality of the novelist himself. Charles Lamb steeped his mind in old writers until some of their quaintness and charm passed into himself and came out in his prose style; and in this way he caught history somehow into his personality. Similarly the historical novelist does not merely acquire information about the past, but absorbs it into his mind. Atmosphere comes out in his books as the overflow of a personality that has made a peculiar appropriation of history. It comes as part of the man himself.

This explains why Hewlett is at home in a peculiarly romantic and coloured world like that of Renaissance Italy, and Dumas is really himself when his books are in an atmosphere of court intrigue and racy adventure, and Scott is a king in his kingdom when he is in the peasant-world of Scotland or when he is concerned with those Covenanting days of which he wrote "I am complete master of the whole history of these strange times." These writers breathe in their novels a life that they have made their own, and that has become part of themselves. It is not a particular period of history but rather a particular phase of life, a certain type of experience, a definite sort of "world" that these writers have come to possess and can so describe with all appropriate atmosphere; and it is not necessarily when they change their period of history but when they move into a different world and concern themselves with a type of life and experience which they have not made their own by any "constant imaginative reference" that they find themselves out of their element. If they take up a fresh corner of life like this for their stories, they are unable to escape from the atmosphere that is really theirs, they cannot shake off the things that belong to the world which is their true world and which has become a part of their thinking; and either they give us no atmosphere at all, or (which is at bottom the same thing) they trail with them into this fresh world an atmosphere which is here alien and inappropriate but which has become part and parcel of themselves.

Moreover, when Hewlett in *King Richard Yea-and-Nay* and Hugo in *Notre Dame de Paris* give us the Middle Ages, although they both achieve a certain atmosphere, it is a different atmosphere in each case. Just as Hugo in *Ninety-Three* reconstructed the French Revolution with his eye upon the conflict between the inexorable demands of the Cause at a moment of crisis and the generous, humane impulses of men who served the cause, he has restored the Middle Ages in *Notre Dame* with his eye upon the Cathedral that is the centre of his story. Wherever he looks he sees a gargoyle; his mind seizes upon the grotesque; and his mediaeval world shapes itself around this central fact.

Hewlett reproduces the Middle Ages as they exist rather in the mind of the poet. Whether he tells of King Richard, or depicts Renaissance times, or relates the story of Mary Queen of Scots, there is always something in his atmosphere that is Hewlett himself, there is a melody in his style, a peculiarity in the very order of his words, that breathes a sort of romance; he gives us the past seen through the coloured windows of his mind. Hugo stands alone as a man who, strikingly aware of the power of accumulated detail, produces atmosphere in a conscious way, knowing what he is doing and how he does it; but he reveals the bent of his mind in the particular appropriation which he makes of the Middle Ages, and in the type of significant fact which he fastens upon. In Hewlett in a more subjective way, there is the mysterious communication of personality. But in every case there is a certain element in atmosphere that is communicated to the past and is imputed to a bygone age by the mind of the man who resurrects the past. His own experience of the past as he has learned to live in it, his own emotions as he looks at some distant century, are transferred to that century. The novelist does not merely reproduce the past any more than an artist merely copies nature; he loads it with something of himself, he cannot describe it without betraying his way of looking at it; and all this is true also of any historian who achieves real resurrection and atmosphere. At its extreme it means a kind of "pathetic fallacy" with a scene in history instead of a scene in nature, shaping itself to the moods and the mind of a man. It is what Carlyle does when he turns to historic men and movements. It is what Turner did when he painted "Ulysses deriding Polyphemus" amid all the glow and colour of legend. It is what the grown-up writer does who gives us children's tales and childhood scenes that seem so charmingly child-like to other grown-ups. It is what all of us do with far-off, remembered things.

And because of all this there is something in the make-up of a historical novelist's mind, something in his temperament and outlook which finds its peculiar home in various corners of the world of the past. There is something in various ages of history, various phases of life and experience, various types of thinking, to which his mind naturally turns, and in which he finds his element. There is something in his own life which answers to its counterpart in history, and finds its own world there. A man like Jokai can catch the atmosphere of some revolutionary movement—as in *The Green Book* —and can thrill a novel with the feelings and the subtle workings of a secret yearning for freedom, because in real life he lived this, and finding it in history found something of himself. Carlyle's Cromwell, Carlyle's Mirabeau have passed through Carlyle's mind and come out crooked; but there was in their way of thinking and in their wrestles with life a thing which Carlyle had in common with them, and which drew his thoughts to them and made their experience a thing he could enter into. That was why he could assimilate them so powerfully to himself. That also was why his interpretations of them were contributions to history, and not mere wild distortions.

And so, for the resurrection of the past and the true re-telling of the life of the past the novelist's peculiar art has something to contribute. The virtue and power of the novelist's depiction of men, is not that he observes perpetually and arranges data, but that he enters into the experiences of others, he runs his life into the mould of their lives, he puts himself under the conditioning circumstances of their thinking. He can feel with people unlike himself and look at the world with their eyes and grapple with the issues of life that meet them, because he can put himself in their place, that is to say, because his experience is not entirely and merely his own. It is precisely because personality is not cut off from personality, and a man is not entirely locked up within himself, with the depths of him completely hidden away from everybody else, that the novelist can so to speak transpose himself and catch life into a person other than himself. It is precisely

because in the last resort a distant age of history
is not its own secret, curled up in its own world,
and cut off from the present day—because the
men of the past had red blood in their veins and
were a phase of a life that is universal and eternal
—that History can recapture something of their
struggles and yearnings and their particular
experiences. The history of history-books gives
us a glimpse of the men of the past, a chart of
the facts that governed their world, an idea of
the conditioning circumstances of their lives;
but it withholds the closest human things, the
touches of direct experience. And because life
is all one, and essential experience ultimately the
same, these are the very things which the novelist,
better than most people, can read back into the
past. These provide the peculiar place, the
legitimate rôle for historical fiction. The novelist
will inevitably colour his pictures of an age with
something of himself, for the pictures are born
of his thinking; but in so far as he does all this
in tune, surprising us with facts that flash, and
that light up the age in unexpected ways, and lure
us into a "world," he will have atmosphere;
and in so far as he remains true to the chart
which history gives him he will have the true
historical atmosphere.

*   *   *   *

The historical novel, then, is one of many
ways of treating the past and of wresting from
it its secret. Given the facts of Nature a scientist

will make one use of them, and will do a certain
kind of thinking around them; but the artist or
the poet will turn a different light upon them
and meet them in a different way. Given the
facts of the past, the historian shapes them in
one way, squeezes something out of them, hunts
out a set of implications in them; the novelist
uses them to a different purpose, organises them
differently, and turns them over in his thinking
with a different kind of logic. Given an event
the historian will seek to estimate its ultimate
significance and to trace out its influence, the
novelist will seek merely to recapture the fleeting
moment, to see the thing happening, to turn
it into a picture or a "situation." With a set
of facts about the social conditions of England
in the Middle Ages the historian will seek to
make a generalisation, to find a formula; the
novelist will seek a different sort of synthesis
and will try to reconstruct a world, to particularise, to catch a glimpse of human nature.
Each will notice different things and follow
different clues; for to the historian the past is
the whole process of development that leads up
to the present; to the novelist it is a strange world
to tell tales about.

Made in the USA
Coppell, TX
26 February 2021